Family Cooking:

Cooking With Family and Friends

Amanda B. Litton

Mutton Cutlets, Breaded.

Trim the cutlets, and season with salt and pepper. Dip in beaten egg and in bread crumbs, and fry in boiling fat. If three-quarters of an inch thick, they will be done rare in six minutes, and well done in ten. Arrange in the centre of a hot dish, and pour tomato sauce around them. One pint of sauce is enough for two pounds of cutlets.

Stewed Steak with Oysters.

Two pounds of rump steak, one pint of oysters, one table-spoonful of lemon juice, three of butter, one of flour, salt, pepper, one cupful of water. Wash the oysters in the water, and drain into a stew-pan. Put this liquor on to heat. As soon as it comes to a boil, skim, and set back. Put the butter in a frying-pan, and when hot, put in the steak. Cook ten minutes. Take up the steak, and stir the flour into the butter remaining in the pan. Stir until a dark brown. Add the oyster liquor, and boil one minute. Season with salt and pepper. Put back the steak, cover the pan, and simmer half an hour; then add the oysters and lemon juice. Boil one minute. Serve on a hot dish with points of toast for a garnish.

Rice Borders.

These are prepared in two ways. The first is to boil the rice as for a vegetable, and, with a spoon, heap it lightly around the edge of the fricassee, ragout, etc. The second method is a little more difficult. Put one cupful of rice on to boil in three cupfuls of cold water. When it has been boiling half an hour, add two table-spoonfuls of butter and one heaping teaspoonful of salt. Set back where it will just simmer, and cook one hour longer. Mash very fine with a spoon, add two well-beaten eggs, and stir for three minutes. Butter a plain border mould, and fill with the rice. Place in the heater for ten minutes. Turn upon a hot dish. Fill the centre with a fricassee, salmis or blanquette, and serve hot. A mould with a border two inches high and wide, and having a space in the centre five and a half inches wide and eleven long, is pretty and convenient for rice and potato borders, and also for jelly borders, with which to decorate salads, boned chicken, creams, etc.

Potato Border.

Six potatoes, three eggs, one table-spoonful of butter, one of salt, half a cupful of boiling milk. Pare, boil and mash the potatoes. When fine and light, add the butter, salt and pepper and two well-beaten eggs. Butter the border mould and pack the potato in it. Let this stand on the kitchen table ten minutes; then turn out on a dish and brush over with one well-beaten egg. Brown in the oven. Fill the centre with a curry, fricassee, salmis or blanquette.

To Make a Crôustade.

The bread for the *crôustade* must not be too light, and should be at least three days old. If the loaf is round, it can be carved into the form of a vase, or if long, into the shape of a boat. Have a very sharp knife, and cut slowly and carefully, leaving the surface as smooth as possible. There are two methods by which it can be browned: one is to plunge it into a deep pot of boiling fat for about one minute; the other is to butter the entire surface of the bread and put it into a hot oven, being careful not to let it burn. Care must be taken that the inside is as brown as the outside; if not, the sauce will soak through the crôustade and spoil it. Creamed oysters, stewed lobster, chicken, or any kind of meat that is served in a sauce, can be served in the crôustade,

Cheese Soufflé.

Two table-spoonfuls of butter, one heaping table-spoonful of flour, half a cupful of milk, one cupful of grated cheese, three eggs, half a teaspoonful of salt, a speck of cayenne. Put the butter in a sauce-pan, and when hot, add the flour, and stir until smooth, but not browned. Add the milk and seasoning. Cook two minutes; then add the yolks of the eggs, well beaten, and the cheese. Set away to cool. When cold, add the whites, beaten to a stiff froth. Turn into a buttered dish, and bake from twenty to twenty-five minutes. Serve the moment it comes from the oven. The dish in which this is baked should hold a quart. An escalop dish is the best.

Rissoles.

Roll the trimmings from pie crust into a sheet about a sixth of an inch thick. Cut this in cakes with the largest patty cutter. Have any kind of meat or fish prepared as for croquettes. Put a heaping teaspoonful on each cake. Brush the edges of the paste with beaten egg, and then fold and press together. When all are done, dip in beaten egg and fry brown in boiling fat. They should cook about eight minutes. Serve hot.

Fritter Batter.

One pint of flour, half a pint of milk, one table-spoonful of salad oil or butter, one teaspoonful of salt, two eggs. Beat the eggs light. Add the milk and salt to them. Pour half of this mixture on the flour, and when beaten light and smooth, add the remainder and the oil. Fry in boiling fat. Sprinkle with sugar, and serve on a hot dish. This batter is nice for all kinds of fritters.

Fritter Batter, No. 2.

One pint of flour, one teaspoonful of salt, one of sugar, one of cream of tartar, half a teaspoonful of soda, one table-spoonful of oil, one egg, half a pint of milk. Mix the flour, salt, sugar, cream of tartar and soda together, and rub through a sieve. Beat the egg very light, and add the milk. Stir half of this on the flour, and when the batter is light and smooth, add the remainder, and finally the oil.

Chicken Fritters.

Cut cold roasted or boiled chicken or fowl in small pieces, and place in an earthen dish. Season well with salt, pepper and the juice of a fresh lemon. Let the meat stand one hour; then make a fritter batter, and stir the pieces into it. Drop, by the spoonful, into boiling fat, and fry till a light brown. Drain, and serve immediately. Any kind of cold meat, if tender, can be used in this way.

Apple Fritters.

Pare and core the apples, and cut in slices about one-third of an inch thick. Dip in the batter, and fry six minutes in boiling fat. Serve on a hot dish. The apples may be sprinkled with sugar and a little nutmeg, and let stand an hour before being fried. In that case, sprinkle them with sugar when you serve them.

Fruit Fritters.

Peaches, pears, pineapples, bananas, etc., either fresh or canned, are used for fritters. If you choose, when making fruit fritters, you can add two table-spoonfuls of sugar to the batter.

Oyster Fritters.

One pint of oysters, two eggs, one pint of flour, one heaping teaspoonful of salt, one table-spoonful of salad oil, enough water with the oyster liquor to make a scant half pint. Drain and chop the oysters. Add the water and salt to the liquor. Pour part of this on the flour, and when smooth, add the remainder. Add the oil and the eggs, well beaten. Stir the oysters into the batter. Drop small spoonfuls of this into boiling fat, and fry until brown. Drain, and serve hot.

Clam Fritters.

Drain and chop a pint of clams, and season with salt and pepper. Make a fritter batter as directed, using, however, a *heaping* pint of flour, as the liquor in the clams thins the batter. Stir the clams into this, and fry in boiling fat.

Cream Fritters.

One pint of milk, the yolks of six, and whites of two, eggs, two table-spoonfuls of sugar, half a pint of flour, three heaping table-spoonfuls of butter, half a teaspoonful of salt, a slight flavoring of lemon, orange, nutmeg, or anything else you please. Put half of the milk on in the double boiler, and mix the flour to a smooth paste with the other half. When the milk boils, stir this into it Cook for five minutes, stirring constantly; then add the butter, sugar, salt and flavoring. Beat the eggs well, and stir them into the boiling mixture. Cook one minute. Butter a shallow cake pan, and pour in the mixture. Have it about half an inch deep in the pan. Set away to cool. When cold, cut into small squares. Dip these in beaten egg and in crumbs, place in the frying basket, and plunge into boiling fat. Fry tall a golden brown. Arrange on a hot dish, sprinkle sugar over them, and serve *very hot*.

Potato Fritters.

One pint of boiled and mashed potato, half a cupful of hot milk, three table-spoonfuls of butter, three of sugar, two eggs, a little nutmeg, one teaspoonful of salt. Add the milk, butter, sugar and seasoning to the mashed potato, and then add the eggs well beaten. Stir until very smooth and light. Spread, about half an inch deep, on a buttered dish, and set away to cool. When cold, cut into squares. Dip in beaten egg and in bread crumbs, and fry brown in boiling fat. Serve immediately.

Croquettes.

Care and practice are required for successfully making croquettes. The meat must be chopped fine, all the ingredients be thoroughly mixed, and the whole mixture be as moist as possible without spoiling the shape. Croquettes are formed in pear, round and cylindrical shapes. The last is the best, as the croquettes can be moister in this form than in the two others.

To shape: Take about a table-spoonful of the mixture, and with both hands, shape in the form of a cylinder. Handle as gently and carefully as if a tender bird. Pressure forces the particles apart, and thus breaks the form. Have a board sprinkled lightly with bread or cracker crumbs, and roll the croquettes *very gently* on this. Remember that the slightest pressure will break them. Let them lie on the board until all are finished, when, if any have become flattened, roll them into shape again. Cover a board *thickly* with crumbs. Have beaten eggs, slightly salted, in a deep plate. Hold a croquette in the left hand, and with a brush, or the right hand, cover it with the egg; then roll in the crumbs. Continue this until they are all crumbed. Place a few at a time in the frying basket (they should not touch each other), and plunge into boiling fat. Cook till a rich brown. It will take about a minute and a half. Take up, and lay on brown paper in a warm pan.

Royal Croquettes.

Three small, or two large, sweetbreads, one boiled chicken, one large table-spoonful of flour, one pint of cream, half a cupful of butter, one table-spoonful of onion juice, one table-spoonful of chopped parsley, one teaspoonful of mace, the juice of half a lemon, and salt and pepper to taste. Let the sweetbreads stand in boiling water five minutes. Chop very fine, with the chicken, and add seasoning. Put two table-spoonfuls of the butter in a stew-pan with the flour. When it bubbles, add the cream, gradually; then add the chopped mixture, and stir until thoroughly heated. Take from the fire, add the lemon juice, and set away to cool. Roll into shape with cracker crumbs. Dip in six beaten eggs and then in cracker crumbs. Let them stand until dry, when dip again in egg, and finally in bread crumbs--not too fine. All the crumbs should first be salted and peppered. Fry quickly in boiling fat.

Royal Croquettes, No. 2.

Half a boiled chicken, one large sweetbread, cleaned, and kept in hot water for five minutes; a calf's brains, washed, and boiled five minutes; one teaspoonful of chopped parsley, salt, pepper, half a pint of cream, one egg, quarter of a cupful of butter, one table-spoonful of corn-starch. Chop the chicken, brains and sweetbread very fine, and add the egg well beaten. Mix the corn-starch with a little of the cream. Have the remainder of the cream boiling, and stir in the mixed corn-starch; then add the butter and the chopped mixture, and stir over the fire until it bubbles. Set aside to cool. Shape, and roll twice in egg and in cracker crumbs. Put in the frying basket, and plunge into boiling fat. They should brown in less than a minute. [Mrs. Furness, of Philadelphia.]

Oyster Croquettes.

Haifa pint of raw oysters, half a pint of cooked veal, one heaping table-spoonful of butter, three table-spoonfuls of cracker crumbs, the yolks of two eggs, one table-spoonful of onion juice. Chop the oysters and veal very fine. Soak the crackers in oyster liquor, and then mix all the ingredients, and shape. Dip in egg and roll in cracker crumbs, and fry as usual. The butter should be softened before the mixing.

Lobster Croquettes.

Chop fine the meat of a two-pound lobster; take also two table-spoonfuls of butter, enough water or cream to make very moist, one egg, salt and pepper to taste, and half a table-spoonful of flour. Cook butter and flour together till they bubble. Add the cream or water (about a scant half cupful), then the lobster and seasoning, and, when hot, the egg well beaten. Set away to cool. Shape, dip in egg and cracker crumbs, and fry as usual.

Salmon Croquettes.

One pound of cooked salmon (about a pint and a half when chopped), one cupful of cream, two table-spoonfuls of butter, one of flour, three eggs, one pint of crumbs, pepper, salt. Chop the salmon fine. Mix the flour and butter together. Let the cream come to a boil, and stir in the flour, butter, salmon and seasoning. Boil for one minute. Stir into it one well-beaten egg, and remove from the fire. When cold, shape, and proceed as for other croquettes.

Shad Roe Croquettes.

One pint of cream, four table-spoonfuls of corn-starch, four shad roe, four table-spoonfuls of butter, one teaspoonful of salt, the juice of two lemons, a slight grating of nutmeg and a speck of cayenne. Boil the roe fifteen minutes in salted water; then drain and mash. Put the cream on to boil. Mix the butter and corn-starch together, and stir into the boiling cream. Add the seasoning and roe. Boil up once, and set away to cool. Shape and fry as directed. [Miss Lizzie Devereux.]

Rice and Meat Croquettes.

One cupful of boiled rice, one cupful of finely-chopped cooked meat--any kind; one teaspoonful of salt, a little pepper, two table-spoonfuls of butter,--half a cupful of milk, one egg. Put the milk on to boil, and add the meat, rice and seasoning. When this boils, add the egg, well beaten; stir one minute. After cooling, shape, dip in egg and crumbs, and fry as before directed.

Rice Croquettes.

One large cupful of cooked rice, half a cupful of milk, one egg, one table-spoonful of sugar, one of butter, half a teaspoonful of salt, a slight grating of nutmeg. Put milk on to boil, and add rice and seasoning. When it boils up, add the egg, well beaten. Stir one minute; then take off and cool. When cold, shape, and roll in egg and crumbs, as directed. Serve very hot. Any flavoring can be substituted for the nutmeg.

Potato Croquettes.

Pare, boil and mash six good-sized potatoes. Add one table-spoonful of butter, two-thirds of a cupful of hot cream or milk, the whites of two eggs, well beaten, and salt and pepper to taste. If you wish, use also a slight grating of nutmeg, or a teaspoonful of lemon juice. Let the mixture cool slightly, then shape, roll in egg and crumbs, and fry.

Chicken Croquettes.

One *solid* pint of finely-chopped cooked chicken, one table-spoonful of salt, half a teaspoonful of pepper, one cupful of cream or chicken stock, one table-spoonful of flour, four eggs, one teaspoonful of onion juice, one table-spoonful of lemon juice, one pint of crumbs, three table-spoonfuls of butter. Put the cream or stock on to boil. Mix the flour and butter together, and stir into the boiling cream; then add the chicken and seasoning. Boil for two minutes, and add two of the eggs, well beaten. Take from the fire immediately, and set away to cool. When cold, shape and fry.

Many people think a teaspoonful of chopped parsley an improvement,

Other Croquettes.

Veal, mutton, lamb, beef and turkey can be prepared in the same manner as chicken. Very dry, tough meat is not suitable for croquettes. Tender roasted pieces give the finest flavor.

Large Vol-au-Vent.

Make puff or chopped paste, according to the rule given, and let it get chilled through; roll it again four times, the last time leaving it a piece about seven inches square. Put in the ice chest for at least half an hour; then roll into a ten-inch square. Place on this a plate or a round tin, nine and a half inches in diameter, and, with a sharp knife, cut around the edge. Place another plate, measuring seven inches or a little more, in the centre. Dip a case-knife in hot water and cut around the plate, having the knife go two-thirds through the paste. Place the paste in a flat baking pan and put in a hot oven. After twelve or fifteen minutes close the drafts, to slacken the heat, and cook half an hour longer, being careful not to let it burn. As soon as the *vol-au-vent* is taken from the oven, lift out the centre piece with a case-knife, and take out the uncooked paste with a spoon. Return the cover. At the time of serving place in the oven to heat through; then fill and cover, and serve while hot The *vol-au-vent* can be made and baked the day before using, if more convenient. Heat it and fill as directed.

Vol-au-Vent of Chicken.

Cut into dice one and a half pints of cooked chicken, and season with salt and pepper. Make a cream sauce, which season well with salt and pepper; and, if you like, add half a teaspoonful of onion juice and the same quantity of mixed mustard. Heat the chicken in this, and fill the *vol-au-vent*. All kinds of poultry and other meats can be used for a *vol-au-vent* with this sauce.

Vol-au-Vent of Sweetbreads.

Clean and wash two sweetbreads, and boil twenty minutes in water to cover. Drain and cool them, and cut into dice. Heat in cream sauce, and fill the *vol-au-vent*. Serve hot.

Vol-au-Vent of Salmon.

Heat one pint and a half of cooked salmon in cream sauce. Fill the *vol-au-vent*, and serve hot. Any rich, delicate fish can be served in a *vol-au-vent*.

Vol-au-Vent of Oysters.

Prepare the vol-au-vent as directed. Put one quart of oysters on to boil in their own liquor. As soon as a scum, rises, skim it off, and drain the oysters.

Return half a pint of the oyster liquor to the sauce-pan. Mix two heaping table-spoonfuls of butter with a scant one of flour, and when light and creamy, gradually turn on it the boiling oyster liquor. Season well with salt, pepper and, if you like, a little nutmeg or mace, (it must be only a "shadow"). Boil up once, and add three table-spoonfuls of cream and the oysters. Stir over the fire for half a minute. Fill the case, cover, and serve immediately.

Vol-au-Vent of Lobster.

Rub together four table-spoonfuls of butter and one and a half of flour. Pour on this, gradually, one pint of boiling white stock. Let it boil up once, and add the juice of half a lemon, salt and a speck of cayenne; add, also, the yolks of two eggs, beaten with a spoonful of cold water, and the meat of two small lobsters, cut into dice. Stir for one minute over the fire. Fill the case, put on the cover, and serve.

Patties.

Make puff paste as directed. (See puff paste.) After it has been rolled four times, put it on ice to harden. When hard, roll again twice. The last time leave the paste about an inch thick. Put in the ice chest to get very firm; then put on the board, and gently roll it down to three-quarters of an inch in thickness. Great care must be taken to have every part equally thick. Cut out pieces with a round tin cutter three and a half inches in diameter, and place in the pans. Take another cutter two and a half inches in diameter, dip it in hot water, place in the centre of the patty, and cut about two-thirds through. In doing this, do not press down directly, but use a rotary motion. These centre pieces, which are to form the covers, easily separate from the rest when baked. Place in a very hot oven. When they have been baking ten minutes close the drafts, to reduce the heat; bake twenty minutes longer. Take from the oven, remove the centre pieces, and, with a teaspoon, dig out the uncooked paste. Fill with prepared fish or meat, put on the covers, and serve. Or, if more convenient to bake them early in the day, or, indeed, the previous day, put them in the oven twelve minutes before serving, and they will be nearly as nice as if fresh baked. The quantities given will make eighteen patties.

Chicken Patties.

Prepare the cream the same as for oysters, and add to it one pint of cold chicken, cut into dice. Boil three minutes. Fill the shells and serve. Where it is liked, one teaspoonful of onion juice is an improvement. Other poultry and all game can be served in patties the same as chicken.

Veal Patties.

Put in a stew-pan a generous half pint of white sauce with a pint of cooked veal, cut into dice, and a teaspoonful of lemon juice. Stir until very hot. Fill the shells, and serve.

Lobster Patties.

One pint of lobster, cut into dice; half a pint of white sauce, a speck of cayenne, one-eighth of a teaspoonful of mustard. Heat all together. Fill the shells and serve.

Oyster Patties.

One pint of small oysters, half a pint of cream, a large tea-spoonful of flour, salt, pepper. Let the cream come to a boil. Mix the flour with a little cold milk, and stir into the boiling cream. Season with salt and pepper. While the cream is cooking let the oysters come to a boil in their own liquor. Skim carefully, and drain off all the liquor. Add the oysters to the cream, and boil up once. Fill the patty shells, and serve. The quantities given are enough for eighteen shells.

Crust Patties.

Cut a loaf of stale bread in slices an inch thick. With the patty cutter, press out as many pieces as you wish patties, and with a smaller cutter, press half through each piece. Place this second cutter as near the centre as possible when using. Put the pieces in the frying basket and plunge into boiling fat for half a minute. Take out and drain, and with a knife, remove the centre crusts and take out the soft bread; then fill, and put on the centre pieces.

Filling for crusts: Put two table-spoonfuls of butter in the frying-pan, and when hot, add one of flour. Stir until smooth and brown. Add one cupful of stock. Boil one minute, and stir in one pint of cooked veal, cut rather fine. Season with salt, pepper, and a little lemon juice. When hot, fill the crusts. Any kind of cold meat can be served in this manner.

Sweetbreads.

Sweetbreads are found in calves and lambs. The demand for calves' sweetbreads has grown wonderfully within the past ten years. In all our large cities they sell at all times of the year for a high price, but in winter and early spring they cost more than twice as much as they do late in the spring and during the summer. The throat and heart sweetbreads are often sold as one, but in winter, when they bring a very high price, the former is sold for the same price as the latter. The throat sweetbread is found immediately below the throat. It has an elongated form, is not so firm and fat, and has not the fine flavor of the heart sweetbread. The heart sweetbread is attached to the last rib, and lies near the heart. The form is somewhat rounded, and it is smooth and firm.

To Clean Sweetbreads.

Carefully pull off all the tough and fibrous skin. Place them in a dish of cold water for ten minutes or more, and they are then ready to be boiled. They must always be boiled twenty minutes, no matter what the mode of cooking is to be.

Sweetbreads Larded and Baked.

When the sweetbreads have been cleaned, draw through each one four very thin pieces of pork (about the size of a match). Drop them into cold water for five or ten minutes, then into hot water, and boil twenty minutes. Take out, spread with butter, dredge with salt, pepper and flour, and bake twenty minutes in a quick oven. Serve with green peas, well drained, seasoned with salt and butter, and heaped in the centre of the dish. Lay the sweetbreads around them, and pour a cream sauce around the edge of the dish. Garnish with parsley. One pint of cream sauce is sufficient for eight or ten sweetbreads.

Sweetbread Sauté.

One sweetbread, after being boiled, split and cut in four pieces. Season with salt and pepper. Put in a small frying-pan one small table-spoonful of butter and the same quantity of flour. When hot, put in the sweetbreads; turn constantly until a light brown. They will fry in about eight minutes. Serve with cream sauce or tomato sauce.

Broiled Sweetbreads.

Split the sweetbread after being boiled. Season with salt and pepper, rub thickly with butter and sprinkle with flour. Broil over a rather quick fire, turning constantly. Cook about ten minutes, and serve with cream sauce.

Breaded Sweetbreads.

After being boiled, split them, and season with salt and pepper; then dip in beaten egg and cracker crumbs. Fry a light brown in hot lard. Serve with tomato sauce.

Sweetbreads in Cases.

Cut the sweetbreads, after being boiled, in very small pieces. Season with salt and pepper, and moisten well with cream sauce. Fill the paper cases, and cover with bread crumbs. Brown, and serve.

Pancakes.

Six eggs, a pint of milk, one heaping teaspoonful of salt, one cupful of flour, one table-spoonful of sugar, one of melted butter or of salad oil. Beat the eggs very light, and add the milk. Pour one-third of this mixture on the flour, and beat until perfectly smooth and light; then add the remainder and the other ingredients. Heat and butter an omelet pan. Pour into it a thin layer of the mixture. When brown on one side, turn, and brown the other. Roll up, sprinkle with sugar, and serve hot. Or, cover with a thin layer of jelly, and roll. A number of them should be served on one dish.

SALADS.

A salad should come to the table fresh and crisp. The garnishes should be of the lightest and freshest kind. Nothing is more out of place than a delicate salad covered with hard-boiled eggs, boiled beets, etc. A salad with which the mayonnaise dressing is used, should have only the delicate white leaves of the celery, or the small leaves from the heart of the lettuce, and these should be arranged in a wreath at the base, with a few tufts here and there on the salad. The contrast between the creamy dressing and the light green is not great, but it is pleasing. In arranging a salad on a dish, or in a bowl, handle it very lightly. Never use pressure to get it into form. When a jelly border is used with salads, some of it should be helped with the salad. The small round radishes may be arranged in the dish with a lettuce salad. In washing lettuce great care must be taken not to break or wilt it. The large, dark green leaves are not nice for salad. As lettuce is not an expensive vegetable, it is best, when the heads are not round and compact, to buy an extra one and throw the large tough leaves away. In winter and early spring, when lettuce is raised in hot-houses, it is liable to have insects on it. Care must be taken that all are washed off. Only the white, crisp parts of celery should be used in salads. The green, tough parts will answer for stews and soups. Vegetable salads can be served for tea and lunch and with, or after, the meats at dinner. The hot cabbage, red cabbage, celery, cucumber and potato salads, are particularly appropriate for serving with meats. The lettuce salad, with the French dressing, and the dressed celery, are the best to serve after the meats. A rich salad, like chicken, lobster or salmon, is out of place at a company dinner. It is best served for suppers and lunches. The success of a salad (after the dressing is made) depends upon keeping the lettuce or celery crisp and not adding meat or dressing to it until the time for serving.

Mayonnaise Dressing.

A table-spoonful of mustard, one of sugar, one-tenth of a teaspoonful of cayenne, one teaspoonful of salt, the yolks of three uncooked eggs, the juice of half a lemon, a quarter of a cupful of vinegar, a pint of oil and a cupful of whipped cream. Beat the yolks and dry ingredients, until they are very light and thick, with either a silver or wooden spoon--or, better still, with a Dover beater of second size. The bowl in which the dressing is made should be set in a pan of ice water during the beating. Add a few drops of oil at a time until the dressing becomes very *thick* and rather hard. After it has reached this stage the oil can be added more rapidly. When it gets so thick that the beater turns hard, add a little vinegar. When the last of the oil and vinegar has been added it should be very thick. Now add the lemon juice and whipped cream, and place on ice for a few hours, unless you are ready to use it. The cream may be omitted without injury.

Salad Dressing Made at the Table.

The yolk of a raw egg, a table-spoonful of mixed mustard, one-fourth of a teaspoonful of salt, six table-spoonfuls of oil. Stir the yolk, mustard and salt together with a fork until they begin to thicken. Add the oil, gradually, stirring all the while. More or less oil can be used.

Cream Salad Dressing.

Two eggs, three table-spoonfuls of vinegar, one of cream, one teaspoonful of sugar, one-fourth of a teaspoonful of salt, one-fourth of a teaspoonful of mustard. Beat two eggs well. Add the sugar, salt and mustard, then the vinegar, and the cream. Place the bowl in a basin of boiling water, and stir until about the thickness of rich cream. If the bowl is thick and the water boils all the time, it will take about five minutes. Cool, and use as needed.

Red Mayonnaise Dressing.

Lobster "coral" is pounded to a powder, rubbed through a sieve, and mixed with mayonnaise dressing. This gives a dressing of a bright color. Or, the juice from boiled beets can be used instead of "coral."

Green Mayonnaise Dressing.

Mix enough spinach green with mayonnaise sauce to give it a bright green color. A little finely-chopped parsley can be added.

Aspic Mayonnaise Dressing.

Melt, but heat only slightly, one cupful of aspic jelly; or, one cupful of consommé will answer, if it is well jellied. Put in a bowl and place in a basin of ice water. Have ready the juice of half a lemon, one cupful of salad oil, one-fourth of a cupful of vinegar, one table-spoonful of sugar, one scant table-spoonful of mustard, one teaspoonful of salt and one-tenth of a teaspoonful of cayenne. Mix the dry ingredients with the vinegar. Beat the jelly with a whisk, and as soon as it begins to thicken, add the oil and vinegar, a little at a time. Add the lemon juice the last thing. You must beat all the time after the bowl is placed in the ice water. This gives a whiter dressing than that made with the yolks of eggs.

Boiled Salad Dressing.

Three eggs, one table-spoonful each of sugar, oil and salt a scant table-spoonful of mustard, a cupful of milk and one of vinegar. Stir oil, salt, mustard and sugar in a bowl until perfectly smooth. Add the eggs, and beat well; then add the vinegar, and finally the milk. Place the bowl in a basin of boiling water, and stir the dressing until it thickens like soft custard. The time of cooking depends upon the thickness of the bowl. If a common white bowl is used, and it is placed in water that is boiling at the time and is kept constantly boiling, from eight to ten minutes will suffice; but if the bowl is very thick, from twelve to fifteen minutes will be needed. The dressing will keep two weeks if bottled tightly and put in a cool place.

Sour Cream Salad Dressing.

One cupful of sour cream, one teaspoonful of salt, a speck of cayenne, one table-spoonful of lemon juice, three of vinegar, one teaspoonful of sugar. Mix all together thoroughly. This is best for vegetables.

Sardine Dressing.

Pound in a mortar, until perfectly smooth, the yolks of four hard-boiled eggs and three sardines, which have been freed of bones, if there were any. Add the mixture to any of the thick dressings, like the mayonnaise or the boiled. This dressing is for fish.

Salad Dressing Without Oil.

The yolks of four uncooked eggs, one table-spoonful of salt, one heaping teaspoonful of sugar, one heaping teaspoonful of mustard, half a cupful of clarified chicken fat, a quarter of a cupful of vinegar, the juice of half a lemon, a speck of cayenne. Make as directed for mayonnaise dressing.

Salad Dressing made with Butter.

Four table-spoonfuls of butter, one of flour, one table-spoonful of salt, one of sugar, one heaping teaspoonful of mustard, a speck of cayenne, one cupful of milk, half a cupful of vinegar, three eggs. Let the butter get hot in a sauce-pan. Add the flour, and stir until smooth, being careful not to brown. Add the milk, and boil up. Place the sauce-pan in another of hot water. Beat the eggs, salt, pepper, sugar and mustard together, and add the vinegar. Stir this into the boiling mixture, and stir until it thickens like soft custard, which will be in about fire minutes. Set away to cool; and when cold, bottle, and place in the ice-chest. This will keep two weeks.

Bacon Salad Dressing.

Two table-spoonfuls of bacon or pork fat, one of flour, one of lemon juice, half a teaspoonful of salt, one teaspoonful of sugar, one of mustard, two eggs, half a cupful of water, half a cupful of vinegar. Have the fat hot. Add the flour, and stir until smooth, but not brown. Add the water, and boil up once. Place the sauce-pan in another of boiling water. Have the eggs and seasoning beaten together. Add the vinegar to the boiling mixture, and stir in the beaten egg. Cook four minutes, stirring all the while. Cool and use. If corked tightly, this will keep two weeks in a cold place.

French Salad Dressing.

Three table-spoonfuls of oil, one of vinegar, one salt-spoonful of salt, one-half a salt-spoonful of pepper. Put the salt and pepper in a cup, and add one table-spoonful of the oil. When thoroughly mixed, add the remainder of the oil and the vinegar. This is dressing enough for a salad for six persons. If you like the flavor of onion, grate a little juice into the dressing. The juice is obtained by first peeling the onion, and then grating with a coarse grater, using a good deal of pressure. Two strokes will give about two drops of juice--enough for this rule.

Chicken Salad.

Have cold roasted or boiled chicken free of skin, fat and bones. Place on a board, and cut in long, thin strips, and cut these into dice. Place in an earthen bowl (there should be two quarts), and season with four table-spoonfuls of vinegar, two of oil, one teaspoonful of salt and one-half of a teaspoonful of pepper. Set away in a cold place for two or three hours. Scrape and wash enough of the tender white celery to make one quart. Cut this, with a sharp knife, in pieces about half an inch thick. Put these in the ice chest until serving time. Make the mayonnaise dressing. Mix the chicken and celery together, and add half of the dressing. Arrange in a salad bowl or on a flat dish, and pour the remainder of the dressing over it. Garnish with white celery leaves. Or, have a jelly border, and arrange the salad in this. Half celery and half lettuce is often used for chicken salad. Many people, when preparing for a large company, use turkey instead of chicken, there being so much more meat in the same number of pounds of the raw material; but the salad is not nearly so nice as with chicken. If, when the chicken or fowl is cooked, it is allowed to cool in the water in which it is boiled, it will be juicier and tenderer than if taken from the water as soon as done.

Lobster Salad.

Cut up and season the lobster the same as chicken. Break the leaves from a head of lettuce, one by one, and wash them singly in a large pan of cold water. Put them in a pan of ice water for about ten minutes, and then shake in a wire basket, to free them of water. Place in the ice chest until serving time. When ready to serve, put two or three leaves together in the form of a shell, and arrange these shells on a flat dish. Mix one-half of the mayonnaise dressing with the lobster. Put a table-spoonful of this in each cluster of leaves. Finish with a teaspoonful of the dressing on each spoonful of lobster. This is an exceedingly inviting dish. Another method is to cut or tear the leaves rather coarse, and mix with the lobster. Garnish the border of the dish with whole leaves. There should be two-thirds lobster to one-third lettuce.

Salmon Salad.

One quart of cooked salmon, two heads of lettuce, two table-spoonfuls of lemon juice, one of vinegar, two of capers, one teaspoonful of salt, one-third of a teaspoonful of pepper, one cupful of mayonnaise dressing, or the French dressing. Break up the salmon with two silver forks. Add to it the salt, pepper, vinegar and lemon juice. Put in the ice chest or some other cold place, for two or three hours. Prepare the lettuce as directed for lobster salad. At serving time, pick out leaves enough to border the dish. Cut or tear the remainder in pieces, and arrange these in the centre of a flat dish. On them heap the salmon lightly, and cover with the dressing. Now sprinkle on the capers. Arrange the whole leaves at the base, and, if you choose, lay one-fourth of a thin slice of lemon on each leaf.

Oyster Salad.

One pint of celery, one quart of oysters, one-third of a cupful of mayonnaise dressing, three table-spoonfuls of vinegar, one of oil, half a teaspoonful of salt, one-eighth of a teaspoonful of pepper, one table-spoonful of lemon juice. Let the oysters come to a boil in their own liquor. Skim well and drain. Season them with the oil, salt, pepper, vinegar and lemon juice. When cold, put in the ice chest for at least two hours. Scrape and wash the whitest and tenderest part of the celery, and, with a sharp knife, cut in *very* thin slices. Put in a bowl with a large lump of ice, and set in the ice chest until serving time. When ready to serve, drain the celery, and mix with the oysters and half of the dressing. Arrange in the dish, pour the remainder of the dressing over, and garnish with white celery leaves.

Sardine Salad.

Arrange one quart of any kind of cooked fish on a bed of crisp lettuce. Split six sardines, and if there are any bones, remove them. Cover the fish with the sardine dressing. Over this put the sardines, having the ends meet in the centre of the dish. At the base, of the dish mate a wreath of thin slices of lemon. Garnish with parsley or lettuce, and serve immediately.

Shad Roe Salad.

Three shad roe, boiled in salted water twenty minutes. When cold, cut in *thin* slices. Season and set away, the same as salmon. Serve the same as salmon, except omit the capers, and use chopped pickled beet.

Salads of Fish.

All kinds of cooked fish can be served in salads. Lettuce is the best green salad to use with them, but all green vegetables, when cooked and cold, can be added to the fish and dressing. The sardine and French dressings are the best to use with fish.

Polish Salad.

One quart of cold game or poultry, cut very fine; the French dressing, four hard-boiled eggs, one large, or two small heads of lettuce. Moisten the meat with the dressing, and let it stand in the ice chest two or three hours. Rub the yolks of the eggs to a powder, and chop the whites very fine. Wash the lettuce and put in the ice chest until serving time. When ready to serve, put the lettuce leaves together and cut in long, narrow strips with a *sharp* knife, or tear it with a fork. Arrange on a dish, heap the meat in the centre, and sprinkle the egg over all.

Beef Salad.

One quart of cold roasted or stewed beef--it must be very tender, double the rule for French dressing, one table-spoonful of chopped parsley, and one of onion juice, to be mixed with the dressing. Cut the meat in *thin* slices, and then into little squares. Place a layer in the salad bowl, sprinkle with parsley and dressing, and continue this until all the meat is used. Garnish with parsley, and keep in a cold place for one of two hours. Any kind of meat can be used instead of beef.

Meat and Potato Salad.

Prepare the meat as directed for beef salad, using, however, one-half the quantity. Add one pint of cold boiled potatoes, cut in thin slices, and dressing. Garnish, and set away as before. These salads can be used as soon as made, but the flavor is improved by their standing an hour or more.

Bouquet Salad.

Four hard-boiled eggs, finely chopped; one head of lettuce, or one pint of water cresses; a large bunch of nasturtium blossoms or buttercups, the French dressing, with the addition of one teaspoonful of sugar. Wash the lettuce or cresses, and throw into ice water. When crisp, take out, and shake out all the water. Cut or tear in pieces. Put a layer in the bowl, with here and there a flower, and sprinkle in half of the egg and half the dressing. Repeat this. Arrange the flowers in a wreath, and put a few in the centre. Serve immediately.

Cauliflower Salad.

Boil one large cauliflower with two quarts of water and one table-spoonful of salt, for half an hour. Take up and drain. When cold, divide into small tufts. Arrange on the centre of a dish and garnish with a border of strips of pickled beet. Pour cream dressing, or a cupful of mayonnaise dressing, over the cauliflower. Arrange a star of the pickled beet in the centre. Serve immediately.

Asparagus Salad.

Boil two bunches of asparagus with one quart of water and one table-spoonful of salt, for twenty minutes. Take up and drain on a sieve. When cold, cut off the tender points, and arrange diem on the dish. Pour on cream salad dressing.

Asparagus and Salmon Salad.

Prepare the asparagus as before directed. Season a quart of cooked salmon with one teaspoonful of salt, one-third of a teaspoonful of pepper, three table-spoonfuls of oil, one of vinegar and two of lemon juice. Let this stand in the ice chest at least two hours. Arrange the salmon in the centre of the dish and the asparagus points around it. Cover the fish with one cupful of mayonnaise dressing. Garnish the dish with points of lemon. Green peas can be used instead of asparagus.

Cucumber Salad.

Cut about one inch off of the point of the cucumber, and pare. (The bitter juice is in the point, and if this is not cut off before paring, the knife carries the flavor all through the cucumber.) Cut in thin slices, cover with cold water, and let stand half an hour. Drain, and season with French dressing. If oil is not liked it can be omitted.

Tomato Salad.

Pare ripe tomatoes (which should be very cold), and cut in thin slices. Arrange on a flat dish. Put one teaspoonful of mayonnaise dressing in the centre of each slice. Place a delicate border of parsley around the dish, and a sprig here and there between the slices of tomato.

Cabbage Salad.

One large head of cabbage, twelve eggs, two small cupfuls of sugar, two teaspoonfuls of salt, one table-spoonful of melted butter, two teaspoonfuls of mustard, one cupful of vinegar, or more, if you like. Divide the cabbage into four pieces, and wash well in cold water. Take off all the wilted leaves and cut out the tough, hard parts. Cut the cabbage very fine with a *sharp* knife. Have the eggs boiled hard, and ten of them chopped fine. Add these and the other ingredients to the cabbage. Arrange on a dish and garnish with the two remaining eggs and pickled beets.

Hot Cabbage Salad.

One quart of finely-shaved cabbage, two table-spoonfuls of bacon or pork fat, two large slices of onion, minced *very fine*; one teaspoonful of salt, one-fourth of a teaspoonful of pepper, half a cupful of vinegar, one teaspoonful of sugar. Pry the onion in the fat until it becomes yellow; then add the other ingredients. Pour the hot mixture on the cabbage. Stir well, and serve at once. Lettuce can be served in the same manner.

Vegetable Salad.

A spoonful of green parsley, chopped fine with a knife; six potatoes, half of a small turnip, half of a carrot, one small beet. Cut the potatoes in small slices, the beet a little finer, and the turnip and carrot very fine. Mix all thoroughly. Sprinkle with a scant teaspoonful of salt--unless the vegetables were salted in cooking, and add the whole French dressing, or half a cupful of the boiled dressing. Keep very cool until served.

Red Vegetable Salad.

One pint of cold boiled potatoes, one pint of cold boiled beets, one pint of uncooked red cabbage, six table-spoonfuls of oil, eight of red vinegar (that in which beets have been pickled), two teaspoonfuls of salt (unless the vegetables have been cooked in salted water), half a teaspoonful of pepper. Cut the potatoes in *thin* slices and the beets fine, and slice the cabbage as thin as possible. Mix all the ingredients. Let stand in a cold place one hour; then serve. Red cabbage and celery may be used together. Use the French dressing.

Potato Salad.

Ten potatoes, cut fine; the French dressing, with four or five drops of onion juice in it, and one table-spoonful of chopped parsley.

Potato Salad, No. 2.

One quart of potatoes, two table-spoonfuls of grated onion, two of chopped parsley, four of chopped beet and enough of any of the dressings to make moist. The sardine is the best for this. Pare and cut the potatoes in thin slices, while hot. Mix the other ingredients with them, and put away in a cool place until serving time. This is better for standing two or three hours.

Cooked Vegetables in Salad.

Nearly every kind of cooked vegetables can be served in salads. They can be served separately or mixed. They must be cold and well drained before the dressing is added. Any of the dressings given, except sardine, can be used.

Dressed Celery.

Scrape and wash the celery. Let it stand in ice water twenty minutes, and shake dry. With a sharp knife, cut it in pieces about an inch long. Put in the ice chest until serving time; then moisten well with mayonnaise dressing. Arrange in the salad bowl or on a flat dish. Garnish with a border of white celery leaves or water-cresses. When served on a flat dish, points of pickled beets, arranged around the base, make an agreeable change.

Lettuce Salad.

Two small, or one large head of lettuce. Break off all the leaves carefully, wash each separately, and throw into a pan of ice water, where they should remain an hour. Put them in a wire basket or coarse towel, and *shake* out all the water. Either cut the leaves with a sharp knife, or tear them in large pieces. Mix the French dressing with them, and serve immediately. Beets, cucumbers, tomatoes, cauliflower, asparagus, etc., can each be served as a salad, with French or boiled dressing. Cold potatoes, beef, mutton or lamb, cut fine, and finished with either dressing, make a good salad.

MEAT AND FISH SAUCES.

Brown Sauce.

One pound of round beef, one pound of veal cut from the lower part of the leg; eight table-spoonfuls of butter, one onion, one large slice of carrot, four cloves, a small piece of mace, five table-spoonfuls of flour, salt and pepper to taste, four quarts of stock. Cut the meat in small pieces. Rub three spoonfuls of the butter on the bottom of a large stew-pan. Put in the meat, and cook half an hour, stirring frequently. Add the vegetables, spice, a bouquet of sweet herbs and one quart of the stock. Simmer this two hours, and add the remainder of the stock. Half a dozen mushrooms will improve the flavor greatly. Put the remainder of the butter in a frying-pan, and when hot, add the flour. Stir until dark brown, and as soon as it begins to boil, add to the sauce. Simmer one hour longer. Season with salt and pepper, and strain through a fine French sieve or gravy strainer. Skim off the fat, and the sauce is ready to use. This will keep a week in winter. It is the foundation for an fine dark sauces, and will well repay for the trouble and expense of making.

White Sauce.

Make the white sauce the same as the brown, but use all veal and white stock. When the butter and flour are cooked together be careful that they do not get browned.

White Sauce, No. 2.

One quart of milk, four table-spoonfuls of butter, four of flour, a small slice of onion, two sprigs of parsley, salt and pepper to taste. Put the milk, onion and parsley on in the double boiler. Mix the butter and flour together until smooth and light. When the milk boils, stir four table-spoonfuls of it into the butter and flour, and when this is well mixed, stir it into the boiling milk. Cook eight minutes. Strain, and serve. This sauce is best with fish.

White Sauce, No. 3.

One large slice of onion, one small slice of carrot, a clove, a small piece of mace, twelve pepper-corns, two table-spoonfuls of flour, two heaping table-spoonfuls of butter, one quart of cream--not very rich, salt to taste. Cook the spice and vegetables slowly in the butter for twenty minutes. Add the flour, and stir until smooth, being careful not to brown. Add the cream, gradually, stirring all the while. Boil for two minutes. Strain, and serve. This sauce is good for veal and chicken cutlets, *quenelles*, sweetbreads, etc.

White Sauce, No. 4.

One pint of milk, one of cream, four table-spoonfuls of flour, the yolks of two eggs, salt and pepper to taste. Put the milk and cream on in the double boiler, reserving one cupful of the milk. Pour eight table-spoonfuls of the milk on the flour, stir until perfectly smooth, and add the remainder of the milk. Stir this into the other milk when it boils. Stir the sauce for two minutes; then cover, and cook eight minutes longer. Season well with salt and pepper. Beat the yolks of the eggs with four spoonfuls of cream or milk. Stir into the sauce, and remove from the fire immediately. The eggs may be omitted, if you choose. One table-spoonful of chopped parsley stirred into the sauce just before taking from the fire, is an improvement. This sauce is nice for all kinds of boiled fish, but particularly for boiled salt fish.

Bechamel Sauce.

One pint of white sauce, one pint of rich cream, salt, pepper. Let the sauce and cream come to a boil separately. Mix them together, and boil up once. Strain, and serve.

Cream Bechamel Sauce.

Three table-spoonfuls of butter, three scant ones of flour, ten pepper-corns, a small piece of mace, half an onion, a large slice of carrot, two cupfuls of white stock, one of cream, salt, a little nutmeg, two sprigs of parsley, one of thyme and one bay leaf. Tie the parsley, bay leaf and thyme together. Rub the butter and flour to a smooth paste. Put all the ingredients, except the cream, in a stew-pan, and simmer half an hour, stirring frequently; add the cream, and boil up once. Strain, and serve.

Allemande Sauce.

One pint of white sauce, the yolks of six eggs, the juice of half a lemon, one table-spoonful of mushroom ketchup, one table-spoonful of butter, half a cupful of cream, salt, pepper, a grating of nutmeg. Let the sauce come to a boil. Place the sauce-pan in another of boiling water, and add all the seasoning except the lemon. Beat the yolks of eggs and the cream together, and add to the sauce. Stir three minutes. Take off, add the lemon juice, and strain.

Cream Sauce.

One pint of cream, one generous table-spoonful of flour, and salt and pepper to taste. Let the cream come to a boil. Have the flour mixed smooth with half a cupful of cold cream, reserved from the pint, and stir it into the boiling cream. Add seasoning, and boil three minutes. This sauce is good for delicate meats, fish and vegetables, and to pour around croquettes and baked and Quaker omelets.

Cream Sauce, No. 2.

One cupful of milk, a teaspoonful of flour and a table-spoonful of butter, salt and pepper. Put the butter in a small frying-pan, and when hot, *but not brown,* add the flour. Stir until smooth; then gradually add the milk. Let it boil up once. Season to taste with salt and pepper, and serve. This is nice to cut cold potatoes into and let them just heat through. They are then creamed potatoes. It also answers as a sauce for other vegetables, omelets, fish and sweetbreads, or, indeed, for anything that requires a white sauce. If you have plenty of cream, use it, and omit the butter.

Polish Sauce.

One pint of stock, two table-spoonfuls of butter, four of grated horseradish, one of flour, one of chopped parsley, the juice of one lemon, one teaspoonful of sugar, salt, pepper. Cook the butter and flour together until smooth, but not brown. Add the stock; and when it boils, add all the other ingredients except the parsley. Boil up once, and add the parsley. This sauce is for roast veal.

Robert Sauce.

Two cupfuls of stock, two small onions, four table-spoonfuls of butter, one heaping table-spoonful of flour, one tea-spoonful of dry mustard, one of sugar, a speck of cayenne, two table-spoonfuls of vinegar, salt. Cut the onions into dice, and put on with the butter. Stir until they begin to color; then add the flour, and stir until brown. As soon as it boils, add the stock and other ingredients, and simmer five minutes. Skim, and serve.

Supreme Sauce.

Add to one pint of white sauce three finely-chopped mushrooms, the juice of half a lemon and one table-spoonful of butter. Simmer all together ten minutes. Rub through the strainer and use.

Olive Sauce.

Two dozen queen olives, one pint of rich stock, the juice of one lemon, two table-spoonfuls of salad oil, one of flour, salt, pepper, a small slice of onion. Let the olives stand in hot water half an hour, to extract the salt. Put the onion and oil in the stew-pan, and as soon as the onion begins to color, add the flour. Stir until smooth, and add the stock. Set back where it will simmer. Pare the olives, round and round, close to the stones, and have the pulp in a single piece. If this is done carefully with a sharp knife, in somewhat the same way that an apple skin is removed whole, the olives will still have their natural shape after the stones are taken out. Put them in the sauce, add the seasoning, and simmer twenty minutes. Skim carefully, and serve. If the sauce is liked thin, half the amount of flour given can be used. This sauce is for roast ducks and other game.

Flemish Sauce.

Cut a cupful of the red part of a carrot into *very small* dice. Cover with boiling water, and simmer one hour. Put three table-spoonfuls of butter, two of flour, a slice of carrot, an onion, cut fine; a blade of mace and twenty pepper-corns in a sauce-pan. Stir over the fire one minute, and add two cupfuls of stock. Simmer gently half an hour. Add a cupful of cream, boil up once, and strain. Now add the cooked carrot, one table-spoonful of chopped parsley, two of chopped cucumber pickles and, if you like, one of grated horseradish. Taste to see if salt enough.

Chestnut Sauce.

One pint of shelled chestnuts, one quart of stock, one teaspoonful of lemon juice, one table-spoonful of flour, two of butter, salt, pepper. Boil the chestnuts in water for about three minutes; then plunge them into cold water, and rub off the dark skins. Put them on to cook with the stock, and boil gently until they will mash readily (it will take about an hour). Mash as fine as possible. Put the butter and flour in a sauce-pan and cook until a dark brown. Stir into the sauce, and cook two minutes. Add the seasoning, and rub all through a sieve. This sauce is for roast turkey. When, to be served with boiled turkey, use only a pint and a half of stock; rub the butter and flour together, and stir into the boiling mixture; rub through the sieve as before; add half a pint of cream to the sauce; return to the fire, boil up once, and serve. The chestnuts used are twice as large as the native fruit All first-class provision dealers and grocers keep them.

Celery Sauce.

Cut the tender parts of a head of celery *very fine*. Pour on water enough to cover them, and no more. Cover the sauce-pan, and set where it will simmer one hour. Mix together two table-spoonfuls of flour and four of butter. When the celery has been boiling one hour, add to it the butter and flour, one pint of milk or cream, and salt and pepper. Boil up once, and serve.

Brown Mushroom Sauce.

One forty-cent can of French mushrooms, two cupfuls of stock, two table-spoonfuls of flour, four of butter, salt, pepper. Melt the butter. Add the flour, and stir until a very dark brown; then gradually add the stock. When this boils up, add the liquor from the mushrooms. Season, and simmer twenty minutes. Skim off any fat that may rise to the top. Add the mushrooms, and simmer five minutes longer. Too much cooking toughens the mushrooms. This sauce is to be served with any kind of roasted, broiled or braised meats. It is especially nice with beef.

Brown Mushroom Sauce, No, 3.

One pint of stock, two cloves, one small slice each of turnip, carrot and onion, three table-spoonfuls of butter, two of flour, half a can of mushrooms, or one-eighth of a pound of the fresh vegetable. Cut the vegetables in small pieces, and fry in the butter with the cloves until brown. Add the flour, and stir until dark brown; then gradually add the stock. Chop the mushrooms, stir into the sauce, and simmer half an hour. Rub through the sieve. Use the same as the other brown mushroom sauce.

White Mushroom Sauce.

Hake a mushroom sauce like the first, using one cupful of white stock and one cupful of cream, and cooking the butter only until smooth. Do not let it become browned.

Beurre Noir.

Two table-spoonfuls of butter, one of vinegar, one of chopped parsley, one teaspoonful of lemon juice, half a tea-spoonful of salt, one quarter of a teaspoonful of pepper. Put the butter in a frying-pan, and when very hot, add the parsley and then the other ingredients. Boil up once. This sauce is for fried and broiled fish, and it is poured over the fish before sending to the table.

Maitre d' Hotel Butter.

Four table-spoonfuls of butter, one of vinegar, one of lemon juice, half a teaspoonful of salt, one quarter of a teaspoonful of pepper, one teaspoonful of chopped parsley. Beat the butter to a cream, and gradually beat in the seasoning. This sauce is spread on fried and broiled meats and fish instead of butter. It is particularly nice for fish and beefsteak.

Maître d' Hôtel Sauce.

One pint of white stock, the yolks of three eggs, one heaping table-spoonful of corn-starch. Put the stock on to boil, reserving one-third of a cupful for the corn-starch. Mix the corn-starch with the cold stock and stir into the boiling. Boil gently for five minutes. Prepare the *maître d' hotel* butter as directed in the rule, and add to it the yolks of the eggs. Gradually stir into this the boiling mixture. After placing the sauce-pan in another of boiling water, stir constantly for three minutes. Take off, and serve.

Hollandaise Sauce.

Half a tea-cupful of butter, the juice of half a lemon, the yolks of two eggs, a speck of cayenne, half a cupful of boiling water, half a teaspoonful of salt. Beat the butter to a cream; then add the yolks, one by one, the lemon juice, pepper and salt. Place the bowl in which these are mixed in a sauce-pan of boiling water. Beat with an egg-beater until the sauce begins to thicken (about a minute), and add the boiling water, beating all the time. When like a soft custard it is done. The bowl, if thin, must be kept over the fire only about five minutes, provided the water boils all the time. The sauce should be poured around meat or fish when it is on the dish.

Lobster Sauce.

One small lobster, four table-spoonfuls of butter, two of flour, one-fifth of a teaspoonful of cayenne, two table-spoonfuls of lemon juice, one pint of boiling water. Cut the meat into dice. Pound the "coral" with one table-spoonful of the butter. Rub the flour and the remainder of the butter to a smooth paste. Add the water, pounded "coral" and butter, and the seasoning. Simmer five minutes, and then strain on the lobster. Boil up once, and serve. This sauce is for all kinds of boiled fish.

Butter Sauce.

Two table-spoonfuls of flour, half a cupful of butter and one pint of boiling water. Work the flour and butter together until light and creamy, and gradually add the boiling water. Stir constantly until it comes to a boil, but do not let it boil. Take from the fire, and serve. A table-spoonful of lemon juice and a speck of cayenne may be added if you choose. A table-spoonful of chopped parsley also gives an agreeable change.

White Oyster Sauce.

One pint of oysters, three table-spoonfuls of butter, one heaping table-spoonful of flour, one of lemon juice, salt, pepper, a speck of cayenne.

Wash the oysters in enough water, with the addition of the oyster liquor, to make a pint. Work the butter and flour to a smooth paste. Let the water and oyster juice come to a boil. Skim, and pour on the flour and butter. Let come to a boil, and add the oysters and seasoning. Boil up once, and serve. Half a cupful of the water may be omitted and half a cupful of boiling cream added at the last moment.

Brown Oyster Sauce.

The same ingredients as for the white sauce. Put the butter and flour in the sauce-pan and stir until a dark brown. Add the skimmed liquor, boil up, and add the other ingredients. Boil up once more, and serve. In the brown sauce stock can be used instead of water. The sauce is served with broiled or stewed beefsteak.

Shrimp Sauce.

Make a butter sauce, and add to it two table-spoonfuls of essence of anchovy and half a pint of canned shrimp. Stir well, and it is ready to serve.

Anchovy Sauce.

Make the butter sauce, and stir into it four table-spoonfuls of essence of anchovy and one of lemon juice.

Egg Sauce.

Six hard-boiled eggs, chopped fine with a silver, knife or spoon; half a cupful of boiling cream or milk, and the butter sauce. Make the sauce, add the boiling cream or milk, and then the eggs. Stir well, and serve.

Fine Herbs Sauce.

One table-spoonful of chopped onion, two of chopped mushroom, one of chopped parsley, two of butter, salt, pepper, one pint of white sauce, No. 3. Put the butter and chopped ingredients in a sauce-pan and stir for one minute over the fire. Add the sauce, and boil up once.

Caper Sauce.

Make a butter sauce, and stir into it one table-spoonful of lemon juice, two of capers, and one of essence of anchovy.

Mustard Sauce.

Stir three table-spoonfuls of mixed mustard and a speck of cayenne into a butter sauce. This is nice for devilled turkey and broiled smoked herrings.

Curry Sauce.

One table-spoonful of butter, one of flour, one teaspoonful of curry powder, one large slice of onion, one large cupful of stock, salt and pepper to taste. Cut the onion fine, and fry brown in the butter.. Add the flour and curry powder. Stir for one minute, add the stock, and season with the salt and pepper. Simmer five minutes; then strain, and serve. This sauce can be served with a broil or *sauté* of meat or fish.

Vinaigrette Sauce.

One teaspoonful of white pepper, one of salt, half a teaspoonful of mustard, half a cupful of vinegar, one table-spoonful of oil. Mix the salt, pepper and mustard together; then *very* slowly add the vinegar, and after mixing well, add the oil. The sauce is to be eaten on cold meats or on fish.

Piquant Sauce.

Two cupfuls of brown sauce, one of consomme, (common stock will do), four table-spoonfuls of vinegar, two of chopped onion, two of chopped capers, two of chopped cucumber pickles, one-fourth of a teaspoonful of cayenne, one teaspoonful of sugar, salt to taste. Cook the onion and vinegar in a sauce-pan for three minutes; then add the sauce, consomme, sugar, salt and pepper. Boil rapidly for five minutes, stirring all the while. Add the capers and pickles, and boil three minutes longer.

Tomato Sauce.

One quart of canned tomatoes, two table-spoonfuls of butter, two of flour, eight cloves and a small slice of onion. Cook the tomato, onion and cloves ten minutes. Heat the butter in a small frying-pan, and add the flour. Stir over the fire until smooth and brown, and then stir into the tomatoes. Cook two minutes. Season to taste with salt and pepper, and rub through a strainer fine enough to keep back the seeds. This sauce is nice for fish, meat and macaroni.

Tartare Sauce.

The yolks of two uncooked eggs, half a cupful of oil, three table-spoonfuls of vinegar, one of mustard, one teaspoonful of sugar, one-quarter of a teaspoonful of pepper, one teaspoonful of salt, one of onion juice, one table-spoonful of chopped capers, one of chopped cucumber pickles. Make the same as mayonnaise dressing. Add the chopped ingredients the last thing. This sauce can be used with fried and broiled meats and fish, and with meats served in jelly.

Champagne Sauce.

Mix thoroughly a table-spoonful of butter with one of flour. Set the sauce-pan on the fire, and stir constantly until the mixture is dark brown; then pour into it half a pint of boiling gravy (the liquor in which pieces of lean meat have boiled until it is very rich). Pour in this gravy slowly, and stir slowly and continually. Let boil up once, season well with pepper and salt, and strain. Add half a cupful of champagne, and serve.

Port Wine Sauce for Game.

Half a tumbler of currant jelly, half a tumbler of port wine, half a tumbler of stock, half a teaspoonful of salt, two table-spoonfuls of lemon juice, four cloves, a speck of cayenne. Simmer the cloves and stock together for half an hour. Strain on the other ingredients, and let all melt together. Part of the gravy from the game may be added to it.

Currant Jelly Sauce.

Three table-spoonfuls of butter, one onion, one bay leaf, one sprig of celery, two table-spoonfuls of vinegar, half a cupful of currant jelly, one table-spoonful of flour, one pint of stock, salt, pepper. Cook the butter and onion until the latter begins to color. Add the flour and herbs. Stir until brown; add the stock, and simmer twenty minutes. Strain, and skim off all the fat. Add the jelly, and stir over the fire until it is melted. Serve with game.

Bread Sauce for Game.

Two cupfuls of milk, one of dried bread crumbs, a quarter of an onion, two table-spoonfuls of butter, and salt and pepper. Dry the bread in a warm oven, and roll into rather coarse crumbs. Sift; and put the fine crumbs which come through, and which make about one-third of a cupful, on to boil with the milk and onion. Boil ten or fifteen minutes, and add a table-spoonful of butter and the seasoning. Skim out the onion. Fry the coarse, crumbs a light brown in the remaining butter, which must be very hot before they are put in. Stir over a hot fire two minutes, being watchful not to burn. Cover the breasts of the roasted birds with these, and serve the sauce poured around the birds, or in a gravy dish.

FORCE-MEAT AND GARNISHES.

Force-Meat for Game.

One pound of clear uncooked veal, a quarter of a pound of fat pork, one pound of boiled ham, one quart of milk, one pint of bread crumbs, half a cupful of butter, three table-spoonfuls of onion juice, one table-spoonful of salt, half a teaspoonful of pepper, six mushrooms, the yolks of four eggs, a speck each of clove, cinnamon, mace and nutmeg. Chop the veal, pork, ham and mushrooms *very fine*, and, with a pestle, pound to a powder. Cook the bread and milk together, stirring often, until the former is soft and smooth. Set away to cool, first adding the butter and seasoning to it. When cold, add to the powdered meat. Mix thoroughly, and rub through a sieve. Add the yolks of the eggs. This force-meat is used for borders in which to serve hot entrees of game. It is also used in game pies, and sometimes for *quenelles*. When used for a border it is put in a well-buttered mould and steamed three hours. It is then turned out on a flat dish, and the hot salmis, blanquette or ragout is poured into the centre.

Ham Force-Meat.

Two pounds of cooked ham, chopped, and then pounded very fine; one pound of bread crumbs, one pint of milk, the yolks of four eggs, one table-spoonful of mixed mustard, one teaspoonful of salt, a speck of cayenne, one cupful of brown sauce. Make as directed for force-meat for game.

Veal Force-Meat.

Three pounds of veal, one cupful of butter, one pint of bread crumbs, one pint of milk, one pint of white sauce, two table-spoonfuls of salt, half a teaspoonful of pepper, two table-spoonfuls of Halford sauce, two of onion juice, the yolks of six eggs, half a teaspoonful of grated nutmeg, two table-spoonfuls of chopped parsley. Make and use the same as game force-meat.

Chicken Force-Meat.

Use only the breast of the chicken. Make the same as veal force-meat, using cream, however, with the bread crumbs, instead of milk. This force-meat is for the most delicate entries only. Either the chicken or veal can be formed into balls about the size of a walnut and fried or poached for soups.

Fish Force-Meat.

This can be made the same as veal force-meat. Salmon and halibut will be found the best kinds of fish to use for it. The force-meat is for entrees of fish.

Force-meat is sometimes formed into a square or oval piece for the centre of the dish. It should be about an inch and a half thick. Place on a buttered sheet or plate and steam two hours. When cooked, slip on to the centre of the dish. Arrange the entree on this, and pour the sauce around the base. Delicate cutlets, sweetbreads, etc., can be used here. Veal or chicken force-meat is the best for all light entrees.

Jelly Border.

Make one quart of aspic jelly. Set the plain border mould (see rice border, under Entries) in a pan with a little ice and water. Pour enough of the liquid jelly into the mould to make a layer half an inch deep. Let this get hard. When hard, decorate with cooked carrot and beet, and the white of a hard-boiled egg. These must all be cut in pretty shapes with the vegetable cutter, and arranged on the jelly. Very carefully add two table-spoonfuls of jelly, and let it harden. Fill with the remainder of the jelly, and set away to harden. At serving time put the mould for half a minute in a pan of warm water. Wipe it, and turn the jelly on a cold flat dish. Fill the centre with salad, boned fowl, or anything else you choose.

Marinade for Fish.

One quart of cider, two slices of carrot, one large onion, four cloves, a bouquet of sweet herbs, two table-spoonfuls of butter, two of salt, half a teaspoonful of pepper and the same quantity of mustard. Cook the onion and carrot in the butter for ten minutes, and add the other ingredients. Cover the sauce-pan, and simmer one hour and a half. This is for stewing fish. It should be strained on the fish, and that should simmer forty minutes.

Cold Marinade.

A bouquet of sweet herbs, the juice of half a lemon, two table-spoonfuls of oil, six of vinegar, one of onion juice, a speck of cayenne, one teaspoonful of salt, one-fourth of a teaspoonful of pepper, one-tenth of a teaspoonful of ground clove. Mix all together. Sprinkle on the meat or fish, which should stand ten or twelve hours. This is particularly for fish, chops, steaks and cutlets which are to be either fried or broiled. Any of the flavorings that are not liked may be omitted. When cooked meats or fish are sprinkled with salt, pepper and vinegar, as for salads, they are said to be marinated.

To Get Onion Juice.

Feel the onion, and grate on a large grater, using a good deal of pressure.

To Fry Parsley.

Wash the parsley, and wipe dry. Put in the frying basket and plunge into boiling fat for half a minute.

To Make Spinach Green.

Wash a peck of spinach. Pour on it two quarts of boiling water. Let it stand one minute. Pour off the water, and pound the spinach to a soft pulp. Put this in a coarse towel and squeeze all the juice into a small frying-pan. (Two people, by using the towel at the same time, will extract the juice more thoroughly than one can.) Put the pan on the fire, and stir until the juice is in the form of curd and whey. Turn this on a sieve, and when all the liquor has been drained off, scrape the dry material from the sieve, and put away for use. Another mode is to put with the juice in the frying-pan three table-spoonfuls of sugar. Let this cook five minutes; then bottle for use. This is really the more convenient way. Spinach green is used for coloring soups, sauces and creams.

Points of Lemon.

Cut fresh lemons in thin slices, and divide these slices into four parts. This gives the points. They are used as a garnish for salads and made dishes.

To Make a Bouquet of Sweet Herbs.

Put two sprigs of parsley on the table, and across them lay two bay leaves, two sprigs of thyme, two of summer savory, and two *leaves* of sage. Tie all the other herbs (which are dry) with the parsley. The bouquet is for soups, stews, game, and meat jellies. When it can be obtained, use tarragon also.

VEGETABLES.

All green vegetables must be washed thoroughly in cold water and dropped into water which has been salted and is just beginning to boil There should be a table-spoonful of salt for every two quarts of water. If the water boils a long time before the vegetables are put in it loses all its gases, and the mineral ingredients are deposited on the bottom and sides of the kettle, so that the water is flat and tasteless: the vegetables will not look green, nor have a fine flavor. The time of boiling green vegetables depends very much upon the age, and how long they have been gathered. The younger and more freshly gathered, the more quickly they are cooked. The following is a time-table for cooking:

Potatoes, boiled.	30 minutes.
Potatoes, baked.	45 minutes.
Sweet Potatoes, boiled.	45 minutes.
Sweet Potatoes, baked.	1 hour.
Squash, boiled.	25 minutes.
Squash, baked.	45 minutes.
Green Peas, boiled.	20 to 40 minutes.
Shell Beans, boiled.	1 hour.
String Beans, boiled.	1 to 2 hours.
Green Corn.	25 minutes to 1 hour.
Asparagus.	15 to 30 minutes.
Tomatoes, fresh.	1 hour.
Tomatoes, canned.	30 minutes.
Cabbage.	45 minutes to 2 hours.
Cauliflower.	1 to 2 hours.
Dandelions.	2 to 3 hours.
Beet Greens.	1 hour.
Onions.	1 to 2 hours.
Turnips, white.	45 minutes to 1 hour.
Turnips, yellow.	1 1/2 to 2 hours.
Parsnips.	1 to 2 hours.
Carrots.	1 to 2 hours.

Nearly all these vegetables are eaten dressed with salt, pepper and butter, but sometimes a small piece of lean pork is boiled with them, and seasons them sufficiently.

Potatoes.

No other vegetable is in America so commonly used and abused. The most inexperienced housekeeper takes it as a matter of course that she or her cook cannot fail of boiling potatoes properly. The time of cooking the potato, unlike that of nearly all other vegetables, does not vary with age or freshness; so there need never be a failure. In baking, the heat of the oven is not always the same, and the time of cooking will vary accordingly. The potato is composed largely of starch. Cooking breaks the cells and sets this starch free. If the potato is removed from heat and moisture as soon as this occurs, it will be dry and mealy, but if it is allowed to boil or bake, even for a few minutes, the starch will absorb the moisture, and the potato will become soggy and have a poor flavor.

Boiled Potatoes.

Twelve medium-sized potatoes, one table-spoonful of salt, boiling water to cover. Pare the potatoes, and if old, let them stand in cold water an hour or two, to freshen them. Boil fifteen minutes; then add the salt, and boil fifteen minutes longer. Pour off *every drop* of water. Take the cover from the sauce-pan and shake the potatoes in a current of cold air (at either the door or window). Place the saucepan on the back part of the stove, and cover with a clean coarse towel until serving time. The sooner the potatoes are served, the better. This rule will ensure perfectly sweet and mealy potatoes, if they were good and ripe at first.

Mashed Potatoes.

Twelve potatoes, one and a half table-spoonfuls of salt, one table-spoonful of butter, half a cupful of boiling milk. Pare and boil as directed for boiled potatoes, and mash fine and light. Add the salt and butter. Beat well; then add the milk, and beat as you would for cake. This will give a light and delicate dish of potatoes. The potatoes must be perfectly smooth before adding the other ingredients.

Purée of Potato.

Prepare the potatoes as directed for mashed potatoes, except use a generous cupful of milk and half a teaspoonful of pepper. If the puree is to serve as a foundation for dry meats, like grouse, veal or turkey, use a cupful of rich stock instead of the milk. This preparation, spread on a hot platter, with any kind of cold meat or fish that has been warmed in a little sauce or gravy, heaped in the centre of it, makes a delightful dish for lunch or dinner.

Potato Puffs.

Prepare the potatoes as directed for mashed potato. While *hot*, shape in balls about the size of an egg. Have a tin sheet well buttered, and place the balls on it. As soon as all are done, brash over with beaten egg. Brown in the oven. When done, slip a knife under them and slide them upon a hot platter. Garnish with parsley, and serve immediately.

Riced Potato.

Have a flat dish and the colander hot. With a spoon, rub mashed potato through the colander on to the hot dish. Be careful that the colander does not touch the potato on the dish. It is best to have only a few spoonfuls of the potato in it at one time. When all has been pressed through, place the dish in the oven for five minutes.

Potato à la Royale.

One pint of hot toiled potatoes, a generous half cupful of cream or milk, two table spoonfuls of butter, the whites of four eggs and yolk of one, salt and pepper to taste. Beat the potato very light and fine. Add the seasoning, milk and butter, and lastly the whites of the eggs, beaten to a stiff froth. Turn into a buttered escalop dish. Smooth with a knife and brush over with the yolk of the egg, which has been well beaten. Brown quickly, and serve. It will take ten minutes to brown. The dish in which it is baked should hold a little more than a quart.

Potatoes à l'Italienne.

Prepare the potatoes as for serving *à la royale*. Add one table-spoonful of onion juice, one of finely-chopped parsley, and half a cupful of finely-chopped cooked ham. Heap lightly in the dish, but do not smooth. Sprinkle on this one table-spoonful of grated Parmesan cheese. Brown quickly, and serve. The cheese may be omitted if not liked.

Thin Fried Potatoes.

Pare and cut raw potatoes *very thin*, with either the vegetable slicer or a sharp knife. Put them in cold water and let them stand in a cold place (the ice chest is best) from ten to twenty-four hours. This draws out the starch. Drain them well. Put about one pint in the frying basket, plunge into boiling lard, and cook about ten minutes. After the first minute set back where the heat will decrease. Drain, and dredge with salt. Continue this until all are fried. Remember that the fat must be hot at first, and when it has regained its heat after the potatoes have been added, must be set back where the potatoes will not cook fast. If the cooking is too rapid they will be brown before they have become crisp. Care must also be taken, when the potatoes are first put in the frying kettle, that the fat does not boil over. Have a fork under the handle of the basket, and if you find that there is danger, lift the basket partly out of the kettle. Continue this until all the water has evaporated; then let the basket remain in the kettle. If many potatoes are cooked in this way for a family, quite an amount of starch can be saved from the water in which they were soaked by pouring off the water and scraping the starch from the bottom of the vessel. Dry, and use as any other starch.

French Fried Potatoes.

Pare small uncooked potatoes. Divide them in halves, and each half in three pieces. Put in the frying basket and cook in boiling fat for ten minutes. Drain, and dredge with salt. Serve hot with chops or beefsteak. Two dozen pieces can be fried at one time.

Potatoes à la Parisienne.

Pare large uncooked potatoes. Cut little balls out of these with the vegetable scoop. Six balls can be cut from one large potato. Drop them in ice water. When all are prepared, drain them, and put in the frying basket. This can be half full each time--that is, about three dozen balls can be put in. Put the basket carefully into the fat, the same as for thin fried potatoes. Cook ten minutes. Drain. Dredge with salt, and serve very hot. These are nice to serve with a fillet of beef, beefsteak, chops or game. They may be arranged on the dish with the meats, or served in a separate dish.

Potato Balls Fried in Butter.

Cut little balls from cooked potatoes with the vegetable scoop. After all the salt has been washed from one cupful of butter (chicken fat will do instead), put this in a small frying-pan. When hot, put in as many potato balls as will cover the bottom, and fry until a golden brown. Take up, drain, and dredge with salt. Serve very hot. These balls can be cut from raw potatoes, boiled in salted water five minutes, and fried in the butter ten minutes. When boiled potatoes are used, the part left after the balls have been cut out, will answer for creamed or Lyonnaise potatoes; but when raw potatoes are used, the part left should be put into cold water until cooking time, and can be used for mashed or riced potatoes.

Potatoes Baked with Roast Beef.

Fare rather small potatoes, and boil for twelve minutes in salted water. Take up and put on the grate with roast beef. Bake twenty-five or thirty minutes. Arrange on the dish with the beef, or, if you prefer, on a separate dish.

Broiled Potatoes.

Cut cold boiled potatoes in slices a third of an inch thick. Dip them in melted butter and *fine* bread crumbs. Place in the double broiler and broil over a fire that is not too hot. Garnish with parsley, and serve on a hot dish. Or, season with salt and pepper, toast till a delicate brown, arrange on a hot dish, and season with butter.

Lyonnaise Potatoes.

One quart of cold boiled potatoes, cut into dice; three table-spoonfuls of butter, one of chopped onion, one of chopped parsley, salt, pepper. Season the potatoes with the salt and pepper. Fry the onions in the butter, and when they turn yellow, add the potatoes. Stir with a fork, being careful not to break them. When hot, add the parsley, and cook two minutes longer. Serve immediately on a hot dish.

Duchess Potatoes.

Cut cold boiled potatoes into cubes. Season well with salt and pepper, and dip in melted butter and lightly in flour. Arrange them on a baking sheet, and bake fifteen minutes in a quick oven. Serve *very hot.*

Housekeeper's Potatoes.

One quart of cold boiled potatoes, cut into dice; one pint of stock, one table-spoonful of chopped parsley, one of butter, one teaspoonful of lemon juice, salt, pepper. Season the potatoes with the salt and pepper, and add the stock. Cover, and simmer twelve minutes. Add lemon juice, butter and parsley, and simmer two minutes longer.

Potatoes à la Maître d' Hôtel.

One quart of cold boiled potatoes, cut into dice; one scant pint of milk, one table-spoonful of chopped parsley, three of butter, one teaspoonful of lemon juice, salt, pepper, the yolks of two eggs, one teaspoonful of flour. Mix the butter, flour, lemon juice, parsley and yolks of eggs together. Season the potatoes with salt and pepper. Add the milk, and put on in the double boiler. Cook five minutes; then add the other ingredients, and cook five minutes longer. Stir often.

Stewed Potatoes.

One quart of cold boiled potatoes, cut into little dice j one pint and a half of milk, one table-spoonful of parsley, one of flour, two of butter, salt, pepper. Put the potatoes in the double boiler, and dredge them with the salt, pepper and flour. Add the parsley, butter and milk. Cover, and put on to boil. Cook twelve minutes. Serve very hot.

Creamed Potatoes.

One quart of cold boiled potatoes, cut in very *thin* slices; one pint of cream sauce, salt, pepper. Season the potatoes with salt and pepper, and turn them into the sauce. Cover the stew-pan, and cook until the potatoes are hot--no longer. Serve immediately in a hot dish. They will heat in the double boiler in six minutes, and will not require stirring.

Escaloped Potatoes.

Cut one quart of cold boiled potatoes in *very thin* slices, and season well with salt and pepper. Butter an escalop dish. Cover the bottom with a layer of cream sauce, add a layer of the potatoes, sprinkle with chopped parsley, and moisten with sauce. Continue this until all the material is used. Have the last layer one of cream sauce. Cover the dish with fine bread crumbs, put a table-spoonful of butter in little bits on the top, and cook twenty minutes. It takes one pint of sauce, one table-spoonful of parsley, half a cupful of bread crumbs, one teaspoonful of salt and as much pepper as you like. This dish can be varied by using a cupful of chopped ham with the potatoes. Indeed, any kind of meat can be used.

Potato Soufflé.

Six large, smooth potatoes, half a cupful of boiling milk, one table-spoonful of butter, the whites of four eggs, salt and pepper to taste. Wash the potatoes clean, being, careful not to break the skin. Bake forty-five minutes. Take the potatoes from the oven, and with a sharp knife, cut them in two, lengthwise. Scoop out the potato with a spoon, and put it in a hot bowl. Mash light and fine. Add the seasoning, butter and milk, and then half the whites of the eggs. Fill the skins with the mixture. Cover with the remaining white of the egg, and brown in the oven. Great care must be taken not to break the skins.

Sweet Potatoes.

Sweet potatoes require from forty-five to fifty-five minutes to boil, and from one hour to one and a quarter to bake. The time given will make the potatoes moist and sweet If, however, they are preferred dry and mealy, fifteen minutes less will be enough.

French Fried Sweet Potatoes.

Prepare and fry the same as the white potatoes. Or, they can first be boiled half an hour, and then pared, cut and fried as directed. The latter is the better way, as they are liable to be a little hard if fried when raw.

Cold Boiled Sweet Potatoes.

Cut cold boiled sweet potatoes in thick slices, and season well with salt and pepper. Have the bottom of the frying-pan covered with either butter, or pork, ham or chicken fat. Put enough of the sliced potatoes in the pan to just cover the bottom. Brown one side, and turn, and brown the other. Serve in a hot dish. Cold potatoes can be served in cream, cut in thick slices and toasted, cut in thick slices, dipped in egg and bread crumbs and fried brown, and can be fried in batter.

Plain Boiled Macaroni.

Two quarts of boiling water, one table-spoonful of salt, and twelve sticks of macaroni. Break and wash the macaroni, throw it into the salt and water, and boil *rapidly* for twenty-five minutes. Pour off the water, season with salt, pepper and butter, and serve.

Macaroni in Gravy.

Twelve sticks of macaroni, one and a half pints of stock, one scant table-spoonful of flour, one generous table-spoonful of butter, salt, pepper. Break and wash the macaroni. Put it in a sauce-pan with the stock. Cover, and simmer half an hour. Mix the butter and flour together. Stir this and the seasoning in with the macaroni. Simmer ten minutes longer, and serve. A table-spoonful of grated cheese may be added.

Macaroni with Cream Sauce.

Boil the macaroni as directed for the plain boiled dish. Drain, and serve with half a pint of cream sauce.

Macaroni with Tomato Sauce.

Boil and drain as directed for plain boiled macaroni. Pour over it one pint of tomato sauce.

Macaroni with Cheese.

Prepare the macaroni with the cream sauce. Turn into a buttered escalop dish. Have half a cupful of grated cheese and half a cupful of bread crumbs mixed. Sprinkle over the macaroni, and place in the oven and brown. It will take about twenty minutes.

Macaroni à l'Italienne.

Twelve sticks of macaroni (a quarter of a pound), half a pint of milk, two table-spoonfuls of cream, two of butter, one of flour, some salt, white pepper and cayenne, and a quarter of a pound of cheese. Break and wash the macaroni, and boil it rapidly for twenty minutes in two quarts of water. Put the milk on in the double boiler. Mix the butter and flour together, and stir into the boiling milk. Add the seasoning, cream and cheese. Drain, and dish the macaroni. Pour the sauce over it, and serve immediately. One table-spoonful of mustard can be stirred into the sauce if you like. If the sauce and macaroni are allowed to stand long after they are put together the dish will be spoiled. If they cannot be served immediately, keep both hot in separate dishes.

Stuffed Tomatoes.

Twelve large, smooth tomatoes, one teaspoonful of salt, a little pepper, one table-spoonful of butter, one of sugar, one cupful of bread crumbs, one teaspoonful of onion juice. Arrange the tomatoes in a baking pan. Cut a thin slice from the smooth end of each. With a small spoon, scoop out as much of the pulp and juice as possible without injuring the shape. When all have been treated in this way, mix the pulp and juice with the other ingredients, and fill the tomatoes with this mixture. Put on the tops, and bake slowly three-quarters of an hour. Slide the cake turner under the tomatoes and lift gently on to a flat dish. Garnish with parsley, and serve.

Stuffed Tomatoes, No 2.

Twelve tomatoes, two cupfuls of bread crumbs, one of stock, four table-spoonfuls of butter, one of flour, salt, pepper, one teaspoonful of onion juice. Cut slices from the stem end of the tomatoes. Remove the juice and pulp with a spoon, and dredge the inside with salt and pepper. Put two table-spoonfuls of the butter in a frying-pan, and when hot, stir in the bread crumbs. Stir constantly until they are brown and crisp, and fill the tomatoes with them. Cover the openings with fresh crumbs and bits of butter. Bake slowly half an hour. Fifteen minutes before the tomatoes are done, make the sauce in this manner: Put one table-spoonful of butter in the frying-pan, and when hot, add the flour. Stir until brown and smooth; then add the stock, tomato juice and pulp. Stir until it boils up, and add the onion juice, salt and pepper. Simmer ten minutes, and strain. Lift the tomatoes on to a flat dish, with the cake turner. Pour the sauce around, garnish with parsley, and serve. Any kind of meat, chopped fine and seasoned highly, can be used in place of the crumbs.

Escaloped Tomatoes.

One pint of fresh or canned tomatoes, one generous pint of bread crumbs, three table-spoonfuls of butter, one of sugar, one scant table-spoonful of salt, one-fourth of a teaspoonful of pepper. Put a layer of the tomato in an escalop dish. Dredge with salt and pepper, and dot butter here and there. Now put in a layer of crumbs. Continue this until all the ingredients are used, having crumbs and butter for the last layer. If fresh tomatoes have been used, bake one hour, but if canned, bake half an hour.

Broiled Tomatoes.

Cut the tomatoes in halves. Sprinkle the inside of the slices with *fine* bread crumbs, salt and pepper. Place them in the double broiler, and broil over the fire for ten minutes, having the outside next the fire. Carefully slip them on a hot dish (stone china), and put bits of butter here and there on each slice. Put the dish in the oven for ten minutes, and then serve. Or, if you have a range or gas stove, brown before the fire or under the gas.

Fried Tomatoes.

Slice ripe tomatoes and dip them in well-beaten eggs, which have been seasoned with salt, pepper and sugar (one teaspoonful of sugar to each egg), and then, in fine bread or cracker crumbs. Have two table-spoonfuls of butter in a frying-pan, and when hot, put in as many slices of tomato as will cover the bottom. Fry for ten minutes, five for each side. Serve on thin slices of toast.

To Peel Tomatoes.

Put the tomatoes in a frying basket and plunge them into boiling water for about three minutes. Drain, and peel.

Baked Onions.

Peel large onions, and boil one hour in plenty of water, slightly salted. Butter a shallow dish or a deep plate, and arrange the onions in it. Sprinkle with pepper and salt, put a teaspoonful of butter in the centre of each onion, and cover lightly with crumbs. Bake slowly one hour. Serve with cream sauce.

Stuffed Onions.

Boil as for baking. Cut out the heart of the onions, and fill the space with any kind of cold meat, chopped fine, and highly seasoned. To each pint of meat add one egg and two-thirds of a cupful of milk or cream. When the onions are filled put a bit of butter (about a teaspoonful) on each one. Cover with crumbs, and bake one hour. Serve with cream sauce.

Parsnips Fried in Butter.

Scrape the parsnips, and boil gently forty-five minutes. When cold, cut in long slices about one-third of an inch thick. Season with salt and pepper. Dip in melted butter and in flour. Have two table-spoonfuls of butter in the frying pan, and as soon as hot, put in enough parsnips to cover the bottom. Fry brown on both sides, and serve on a hot dish.

Parsnips Fried in Molasses.

Have one cupful of molasses in a large frying-pan. When boiling, put in slices of parsnips that have been seasoned with salt, and cooled. Fry brown, and serve hot.

Parsnip Balls.

Mash one pint of boiled parsnips. Add two table-spoonfuls of butter, one heaping teaspoonful of salt, a little pepper, two table-spoonfuls of cream or milk and one beaten egg. Mix all the ingredients except the egg. Stir on the fire until the mixture bubbles; then add the egg, and set away to cool. When cold, make into balls one-third the size of an egg. Dip them in beaten egg and in crumbs. Put in the frying basket and plunge into boiling fat. Cook till a rich brown.

Escaloped Parsnip.

Prepare the parsnips as for the balls, omitting the egg. Turn into a buttered dish, cover with crumbs, dot with butter, and brown in the oven.

Asparagus with Cream.

Have the asparagus tied in bundles. Wash, and plunge into boiling water in which there is a teaspoonful of salt for every quart of water. Boil rapidly for fifteen minutes. Take up, and cut off the tender heads. Put them in a clean sauce-pan with one generous cupful of cream or milk to every quart of asparagus. Simmer ten minutes. Mix one table-spoonful of butter and a generous teaspoonful of flour together. When creamy, stir in with the asparagus. Add salt and pepper to taste, and simmer five minutes longer.

Green, Peas à la Française.

Boil green peas until tender, and drain. For every quart, put in a sauce-pan two table-spoonfuls of butter, one of flour, and half a teaspoonful of sugar. Stir until all are thoroughly mixed. Add the peas, and stir over the fire for five minutes. Add one cupful of white stock or cream, and simmer ten minutes. The canned peas can be prepared in the same manner.

Minced Cabbage.

Drain boiled cabbage in the colander. Put it in the chopping tray and chop fine. For each quart of the chopped cabbage, put two table-spoonfuls of butter and one of flour in the frying-pan. As soon as smooth and hot, put in the cabbage, which season well with salt, pepper, and, if you like it, two table-spoonfuls of vinegar. Stir constantly for five or eight minutes. When done, heap on a dish. Make smooth with a knife, and garnish with hard-boiled eggs.

Minced Spinach.

Boil the spinach in salt and water until tender. Drain in the colander, and chop fine in the tray. Season well with pepper and salt. For each quart of the chopped spinach, put two table-spoonfuls of butter and one of flour in a frying-pan. When this has cooked smooth, and before it has become browned, add the spinach. Stir for five minutes; then add half a cupful of cream or milk, and stir three minutes longer. Arrange in a mound on a hot dish. Garnish with a wreath of slices of hard-boiled eggs at the base, and finish the top with another wreath. Serve hot. Lettuce can be cooked and served in the same manner. It must be boiled about twenty minutes to be tender.

Cauliflower with Cream Sauce.

Take off the green leaves and the stalk of the cauliflower. Wash, and put on to cook in boiling water. Boil gently for half an hour. Turn off the water, and add one pint of milk, one pint of boiling water and one table-spoonful of salt. Simmer half an hour longer. Take up with, a skimmer, being careful not to break it. Pour over this a cream sauce, and serve.

Escaloped Cauliflower.

Cook the cauliflower one hour in salt and water. Drain, and break apart. Put a layer of the cauliflower in an escalop dish, moisten it with Bechamel or cream sauce, and sprinkle in a little grated cheese. Put in another layer of cauliflower, and continue, as directed before, until all of the vegetable is used. There should be two table-spoonfuls of grated cheese and one pint of sauce to each head of cauliflower. Cover with bread crumbs and cheese, and dot with bits of batter. Bake half an hour in a moderate oven.

Stewed Celery with Cream Sauce.

Wash and scrape the tender white part of two heads of celery. Cut them in pieces about two inches long. Cover with boiling water and simmer gently half an hour. Season well with salt. Drain off the water in which the celery was cooked. Add a pint of cream sauce, and serve.

Celery Stewed in Stock.

Scrape, wash and cut the white part of two heads of celery. Put in a stew-pan with one pint of stock, and simmer half an hour. Mix together two table-spoonfuls of butter and one of flour. Stir this in with the celery. Season with salt, and simmer five minutes longer.

Stewed Okra.

After the ends of the pods have been cut off, wash, and put on with just enough water to prevent burning (about a cupful to a quart of the okra) and a teaspoonful of salt. Simmer gently thirty minutes. Season with pepper and butter, and with more salt, if necessary.

Okra Stewed with Tomatoes.

Cut the okra in thin slices, and pare and slice the tomatoes. Have one pint of tomatoes to two of okra. Put the vegetables in a stew-pan with one teaspoonful of salt and a little pepper. Simmer half an hour. Add one table-spoonful of butter, and more salt, if needed.

Scalloped Okra and Tomatoes.

Prepare the same as stewed okra and tomatoes. When they have been stewing fifteen minutes add the butter and pepper, and turn into a deep dish. Cover with bread or cracker crumbs, dot with butter, and bake half an hour.

Fried Egg Plant.

Cut the plant in slices about one-third of an inch thick. Pare these, and lay in a flat dish. Cover with boiling water, to which has been added one table-spoonful of salt for every quart of water. Let this stand one hour. Drain, and pepper the slices slightly, and dip in beaten egg and bread crumbs (two eggs and a pint of crumbs for a good-sized plant). Fry in boiling fat for eight or ten minutes. The slices will be soft and moist when done. Or, the slices can be seasoned with pepper, and fried in just enough pork fat to brown them. The egg plant is sometimes stewed, and sometimes baked, but there is no other mode so good as frying.

Boiled Rice.

One cupful of rice, one quart of boiling water, one scant table-spoonful of salt. Wash the rice in three waters, and put in the double kettle with the salt and boiling water. Boil rapidly fifteen minutes; then pour off *all* the water. Cover tightly, return to the fire, and cook twenty minutes longer. The water in the under boiler must boil rapidly all the time. Rice cooked in this manner will have every grain separate.

Corn Oysters.

One cupful of flour, half a cupful of melted butter, three table-spoonfuls of milk, two teaspoonfuls of salt, one-fourth of a teaspoonful of pepper, one pint of grated corn. Pour the corn on the flour, and beat well; then add the other ingredients, and beat rapidly for three minutes. Have fat in the frying-pan to the depth of about two inches. When smoking hot, put in the batter by the spoonful. Hold the spoon close to the fat and the shape of the oyster will be good. Fry about five minutes.

New Bedford Corn Pudding.

Twelve ears of corn, four eggs, a generous pint and a half of milk, a generous teaspoonful of salt, four table-spoonfuls of sugar. Grate the corn, beat the eggs with a spoon, and mix all the ingredients together. Butter a deep earthen dish, and pour the mixture into it. Bake slowly two hours. Serve hot. When the corn is old it will take one quart of milk. If very young and milky, one pint of milk will be sufficient.

Pickled Beets.

Cut boiled beets in slices. Lay these in a large glass jar or earthen pot. For every beet, put in one slice of onion, one table-spoonful of grated horse-radish, six cloves, and vinegar enough to cover. The beets will be ready to use in ten or twelve hours. They will not keep more than a week.

Baked Beans.

Pick one quart of beans free from stones and dirt. Wash, and soak in cold water over night. In the morning pour off the water. Cover with hot water, put two pounds of corned beef with them, and boil until they begin to split open, (the time depends upon the age of the beans, but it will be from thirty to sixty minutes). Turn them into the colander, and pour over them two or three quarts of cold water. Put about half of the beans in a deep earthen pot, then put in the beef, and finally the remainder of the beans. Mix one tea-spoonful of mustard and one table-spoonful of molasses with a little water. Pour this over the beans, and then add boiling water to just cover. Bake *slowly* ten hours. Add a little water occasionally.

PIES AND PUDDINGS.

Puff Paste.

One quart of pastry flour, one pint of butter, one table-spoonful of salt, one of sugar, one and a quarter cupfuls of ice water. Wash the hands with soap and water, and dip them first in very hot, and then in cold, water. Rinse a large bowl or pan with boiling water and then with cold. Half fill it with cold water. Wash the butter in this, working it with the hands until it is light and waxy. This frees it of the salt and butter-milk, and lightens it, so that the pastry is more delicate. Shape the butter into two thin cakes, and put in a pan of ice water, to harden. Mix the salt and sugar with the flour. With the hands, rub one-third of the butter into the flour. Add the water, stirring with a knife. Stir quickly and vigorously until the paste is a smooth ball. Sprinkle the board *lightly* with flour. Turn the paste on this, and pound quickly and lightly with the rolling pin. Do not break the paste. Roll from you and to one side; or, if easier to roll from you all the while, turn the paste around. When it is about one-fourth of an inch thick, wipe the remaining butter, break it in bits, and spread these on the paste. Sprinkle lightly with flour. Fold the paste, one-third from each side, so that the edges meet. Now fold from the ends, but do not have these meet. Double the paste, pound lightly, and roll down to about one-third of an inch in thickness. Fold as before, and roll down again. Repeat this three times if for pies, and six times if for *vol-au-vents*, patties, tarts, etc. Place on the ice, to harden, when it has been rolled the last time. It should be in the ice chest at least an hour before being used. In hot weather if the paste sticks when being rolled down, put it on a tin sheet and place on ice. As soon as it is chilled it will roll easily. The less flour you use in rolling out the paste the tenderer it will be. No matter how carefully every part of the work may be done, the paste will not be good if much flour is used.

Chopped Paste.

One quart of pastry flour, two cupfuls of unwashed butter, one teaspoonful of salt, one table-spoonful of sugar, and a scant cupful of ice water. Put the flour, salt, sugar and butter in the chopping-tray. Chop all together until the butter is thoroughly mixed with the flour; then add the water, and continue chopping. When well mixed, sprinkle the board with flour, turn the paste on it, and roll into a flat piece. Place in a pan on the ice. When hard, use the same as puff paste. It can be used as soon as mixed, but will not, of course, be so nice.

French Paste for Raised Pies.

One quart of pastry flour, one table-spoonful of sugar, one teaspoonful of salt, one scant cupful of butter, one egg, one tea-cupful of water. Rub the butter, salt and sugar into the flour. Beat the egg, and add the water to it. Stir this into the flour and butter. Stir this mixture until it is a smooth paste; then put on the board and roll the same as puff paste. This paste must be rolled eight times.

To Make a Pie.

Butter the pie plate (tin is the best), and cover with paste that has been rolled very thin. Roll a strip of paste long enough to go around the plate, and cut in strips an inch wide. Wet the edge of the plate with water, and put a strip of paste on it. Fill with any kind of prepared fruit Have the paste in a roll, and cut enough from the end to cover the pie. Sprinkle the board lightly with flour, and place the paste up-on it. Flour the rolling pin with, the hand. Roll from you and to one side until the paste is the right size. It must be much larger than the plate. In the centre cut a slit about halt an inch long. Cover the pie, having the paste "*fulled*" on, as it shrinks in the baking. The oven must be hot at first, and after the first fifteen minutes the drafts must be closed. A mince pie will require one hour to bake, and an apple pie fifty minutes. Peach, and nearly all other fruit pies, require the same time.

Mince Pie Meat.

Boil a beef tongue, weighing six pounds, and six pounds of the vein of a round of beef (these should just simmer). After skinning the tongue, chop it and the beef very fine, and add five pounds of beef suet, chopped fine; five pounds of stoned raisins, three of dried currants, one and a half of citron, cut fine; nine of sugar, one and a half pints of molasses, two quarts of the liquor in which the meat was boiled, one quart of brandy, one pint of white wine, a cupful of salt, half a cupful of cinnamon, one-fourth of a cupful of cloves, one-fourth of a cupful of allspice, three nutmegs, a table-spoonful of mace. Put all in a large pan, and let stand over night. Put what you wish to bake in another pan with half as much stewed and sweetened apple as you have meat, and let it stand one hour. Put the remainder of the meat in a jar. Cover with a paper dipped in brandy, and then cover tightly, to exclude the air. Set in a cool place for future use, [Mrs. M. L. W.]

Squash pies.

Five pints of stewed and strained squash, two quarts of boiling milk, one and a half nutmegs, four teaspoonfuls of salt, five cupfuls of sugar, nine eggs, four table-spoonfuls of Sicily Madeira and two of rose-water. Gradually pour the boiling milk on the squash, and stir continually. Add the nutmeg, rose-water and sugar. When cold, add the eggs, well beaten; and just before the mixture is put in the plates, add the Madeira. Butter deep plates, and line with a plain paste. Fill with the mixture, and bake in a moderate oven for forty minutes. [Mrs. M. L. W.]

Sweet Potato Pies.

When the potatoes are dry and mealy, take a quart after they have been pared, boiled and mashed, a quart of milk, four eggs, salt, nutmeg, cinnamon and sugar to taste. Bake the same as squash pies. If the potatoes are very moist, use less milk.

Lemon Pie.

The juice and rind of one lemon, two eggs, eight heaping table-spoonfuls of sugar, one small tea-cupful of milk, one teaspoonful of corn-starch. Mix the corn-starch with a little of the milk. Put the remainder on the fire, and when boiling, stir in the corn-starch. Boil one minute. Let this cool, and add the yolks of the eggs, four heaping table-spoonfuls of the sugar, and the grated rind and juice of the lemon, all well beaten together. Have a deep pie plate lined with paste, and fill with this mixture. Bake slowly half an hour. Beat the whites of the eggs to a stiff froth, and gradually beat into them the remainder of the sugar. Cover the pie with this, and brown slowly.

Orange Pies.

Two cupfuls of sugar, two of flour, five eggs, one tea-spoonful of cream of tartar, half a teaspoonful of soda, the juice and rind of one orange. These are for the cake. Beat the eggs very light; then add the sugar, and beat until frothy. Now add the orange. Mix the soda and cream of tartar with the flour, and rub through a sieve on to the beaten eggs and sugar. Stir well, and bake in deep tin plates. There will be enough for six plates. When baked, put a thin layer of the icing between the cakes, and cover the pie with icing. There should be three cakes in a pie. Icing: The whites of four eggs, one tea-cupful of powdered sugar, the juice and rind of two oranges. After beating the whites to a stiff froth, beat in the sugar and then the rind and juice of the oranges. When the pies are iced, dry them in the heater.

Chocolate Pies.

Make plain cup cake, and bake in Washington-pie plates, having the cake thick enough to split. After splitting, spread one half with a filling made as below, place the top piece on, and sprinkle with powdered sugar. The cake should always be fresh.

Filling: One square of Baker's chocolate, one cupful of sugar, the yolks of two eggs, one-third of a cupful of boiling milk. Mix scraped chocolate and sugar together; then add, very slowly, the boiling milk, and then the eggs, and simmer ten minutes, being careful that it does not burn. Flavor with vanilla. Have fully cold before using.

HOT PUDDINGS.

Custard Soufflé.

Two scant table-spoonfuls of butter, two table-spoonfuls of flour, two table-spoonfuls of sugar, one cupful of milk, four eggs. Let the milk come to a boil. Beat the flour and butter together; add to them, gradually, the boiling milk, and cook eight minutes, stirring often. Beat the sugar and the yolks of the eggs together. Add to the cooked mixture, and set away to cool. When cool, beat the whites of the eggs to a stiff froth, and add to the mixture. Bake in a buttered pudding dish for twenty minutes in a moderate oven. Serve *immediately* with creamy sauce.

Cabinet Pudding.

One quart of milk, four eggs, four table-spoonfuls of sugar, half a teaspoonful of salt, one table-spoonful of butter, three pints of stale sponge cake, one cupful of raisins, chopped citron and currants. Have a little more of the currants than of the two other fruits. Beat the eggs, sugar and salt together, and add the milk. Butter a three-pint pudding mould (the melon shape is nice), sprinkle the sides and bottom with the fruit, and put in a layer of cake. Again sprinkle in fruit, and put in more cake. Continue this until all the materials are used. Gradually pour on the custard. Let the pudding stand two hours, and steam an hour and a quarter. Serve with wine or creamy sauce.

English Plum Pudding.

A pound of suet, chopped fine; a pint of sugar, one pound of grated stale bread, one pound of raisins, two of currants, a glass of brandy, two teaspoonfuls of ginger, two nutmegs, half a pint of milk, a little salt Beat well, and steam five hours. Serve with rich sauce.

Rachel Pudding.

One quart of breadcrumbs, one of apples, cut very fine; half a cupful of suet, chopped very fine; one cupful of English currants, the rind and juice of two lemons, four eggs, well beaten. Mix thoroughly. Grease a pudding mould, and put the mixture in it. Steam three hours, and serve with rich wine sauce.

Chocolate Pudding.

One quart of milk, four table-spoonfuls of corn-starch, four of sugar, four of scraped chocolate, two of boiling water, two eggs, one teaspoonful of salt. Reserve one cupful of the milk, and put the remainder on to boil. Put the sugar, chocolate and water in a sauce-pan or, better still, a small frying-pan, and stir over a *hot* fire for about a minute, when the mixture should be smooth and glossy. Stir this into the boiling milk. Mix the corn-starch with cold milk. Beat the egg, and add to the corn-starch and milk; add, also, the salt. Stir this into the *boiling* milk, and beat well for about three minutes. Turn the mixture into a melon mould that has been dipped in cold water. Let the pudding stand in the mould about fifteen minutes. Turn into the pudding dish, and heap whipped cream around it. Serve sugar and cream with it; or, vanilla sauce will answer.

Chocolate Roll Pudding.

This pudding consists of cake, frosting and sauce. It is very nice. Beat the whites of three eggs to a stiff froth, and add the yolks. Beat into the eggs one cupful of sugar and one of flour. As soon as all are thoroughly mixed, stir in half a cupful of cold water, in which has been dissolved soda about the size of a pea. Pour thin into a buttered pan, and bake in a moderate oven from twelve to fifteen minutes. When baked, sprinkle the top with two table-spoonfuls of milk.

Frosting: Beat the whites of six eggs to a froth, and divide into two parts. Put a teaspoonful of sugar to one half, and one teaspoonful of sugar and three of grated chocolate to the other. Take the cake from the pan and put it on a flat dish or tin sheet. Spread half of each mixture over the top. Return to the oven for about five minutes, to harden the frosting. Take out and roll up. Put the remainder of the frosting on the top and sides of the roll. Put again in the oven to harden the frosting. Take out, and slide on a flat dish. Pour the sauce around, and serve. The yolks of the eggs may be used for puddings or custards.

Sauce: One egg, one tea-cupful of powdered sugar, five table-spoonfuls of boiling milk, one teaspoonful of vanilla extract. Beat the white of the egg to a stiff froth, and gradually beat in the sugar. Add the yolk of the egg, the vanilla, and lastly the boiling milk.

Ground Rice Pudding.

One quart of milk, five table-spoonfuls of ground rice, four of sugar, one teaspoonful of salt, six eggs, half a cupful of butter. Put the milk in the double boiler, reserving half a cupful. Mix the rice and cold milk together, and stir into the milk in the boiler when this is hot. Stir constantly for five minutes. Add the salt, butter and sugar, and set away to cool. When cold, add the eggs, well beaten. Bake one hour in a moderate oven. Serve with creamy sauce.

Rice Pudding.

One cupful of rice, one quart of milk, one cupful of raisins, one heaping teaspoonful of salt, one cupful of water, one quart of soft custard. Wash the rice, and let it soak two hours in cold water. Turn off the water, and put the rice in the double boiler with the cupful of water. Cook half an hour; then add the salt, raisins and milk, and cook an hour longer. Butter a melon mould and pack the rice in it. Let it stand twenty minutes. Turn out on a deep dish, decorate with bits of bright jelly, pour the custard around, and serve. The custard should be *cold* and the pudding *hot*. The raisins can be omitted if not liked.

German Puffs.

The yolks of six eggs, five table-spoonfuls of flour, one of melted butter, one pint of milk, half a teaspoonful of salt. Beat the yolks of the eggs light, add the milk to them, and pour part of this mixture on the flour. Beat light and smooth; then add the remainder of the eggs and milk, and the salt and butter. Butter muffin pans, and half fill them with the batter. The quantities given will make twelve puffs. Bake twenty minutes in a quick oven. Serve on a hot platter with the sauce poured over them.

Sauce: The whites of six eggs, one cupful of powdered sugar, the juice of two oranges or of one lemon. After beating the whites to a stiff froth, gradually beat in the sugar, and then the juice of the fruit.

Down-East Pudding.

One pint of molasses, one quart of flour, one table-spoonful of salt, one teaspoonful of soda, three pints of blackberries. Boil three hours, and serve with sauce made in the following manner:

One tea-cupful of powdered sugar, half a cupful of butter, one egg, two teaspoonfuls of *boiling* water, one of brandy. Beat the butter to a cream, and add, very gradually, the sugar and brandy. Beat in the yolk of the egg, and, when perfectly creamy, add the white, which has been beaten to a froth; then add the water, and stir very carefully.

Amber Pudding.

One dozen large, tart apples, one cupful of sugar, the juice and rind of two lemons, six eggs, four table-spoonfuls of butter, enough puff or chopped paste to line a three-pint pudding dish. Pare and quarter the apples. Pare the thin rind from the lemon, being careful not to cut into the white part. Put the butter, apple, and lemon rind and juice in a stew-pan with half a cupful of water. Cover tightly, and simmer about three-quarters of an hour. Rub through a sieve, add the sugar, and set away to cool. Line the dish with *thin* paste. Beat the yolks of the eggs, and stir into the cooled mixture. Turn this into the lined dish. Bake slowly for half an hour. Beat the whites to a stiff froth, and gradually beat into them three table-spoonfuls of powdered sugar. Cover the pudding with this. Return to the oven and cook twelve minutes with the door open. Serve either hot or cold.

Fig Pudding.

One cupful of molasses, one of chopped suet, one of milk, three and a quarter of flour, two eggs, one teaspoonful of soda, one of cinnamon, half a teaspoonful of nutmeg, one pint of figs. Mix together the molasses, suet, spice, and the figs, cut fine. Dissolve the soda with a table-spoonful of hot water, and mix with the milk. Add to the other ingredients. Beat the eggs light, and stir into the mixture. Add the flour, and beat thoroughly. Butter two small or one large brown bread mould. Turn the mixture into the mould or moulds, and steam five hours. Serve with creamy or wine sauce.

Date Pudding.

Make the same as fig pudding, but use a pint of dates instead of the figs.

Apple Tapioca Pudding.

One large cupful of tapioca, three pints of water, one cupful of sugar, one teaspoonful of salt, one teaspoonful of essence of lemon, three pints of pared and quartered apples. Wash the tapioca and soak over night in three pints of cold water (three hours will do if there is no more time). Put the tapioca in the double boiler and cook until it looks clear. It will take from twenty to thirty minutes. When cooked enough, add the sugar, salt and lemon, and then the apples. Turn into a buttered dish and bake an hour and a quarter. Let it stand in a cool room half an hour before serving. Serve with sugar and cream.

Baked Apple Pudding.

Fill a three-quart earthen dish with pared and quartered apples. Sprinkle on these one cupful of sugar, a slight grating of nutmeg, one table-spoonful of butter, and half a cupful of water. Cover, and bake thirty minutes. Make half the rule for chopped paste. Roll a piece of the paste into a strip that will reach around the pudding dish. This strip should be about two inches deep. Roll the remainder of the paste to cover the dish. Take the pudding dish from the oven, slip the strip of paste between the apple and the dish, and put on the top crust. Return to the oven, and bake one hour longer. Serve with a cream sauce.

Dutch Apple Pudding.

One pint of flour, one teaspoonful of cream of tartar, half a teaspoonful of soda, half a teaspoonful of salt, an egg, a generous two-thirds of a cupful of milk, two table-spoonfuls of butter, four large apples. Mix the salt, soda and cream of tartar with the flour, and rub through the sieve. Beat the egg light, and add the milk. Rub the butter into the flour. Pour the milk and egg on this, and mix quickly and thoroughly. Spread the dough about half an inch deep on a buttered baking pan. Have the apples pared, cored and cut into eighths. Stick these pieces in rows into the dough. Sprinkle with two table-spoonfuls of sugar. Bake in a quick oven for about twenty-five minutes. This pudding is to be eaten with sugar and cream or a simple sauce.

Apple Soufflé.

One pint of steamed apple, one table-spoonful of melted butter, half a cupful of sugar, the whites of six eggs and the yolks of three, a slight grating of nutmeg. Stir into the hot apple the butter, sugar and nutmeg, and the yolks of the eggs, well beaten. When this is cold, beat the whites of the eggs to a stiff froth, and stir into the mixture. Butter a three-pint dish, and turn the *soufflé* into it. Bake thirty minutes in a moderate oven. Serve immediately with any kind of sauce.

Apple and Rice Pudding.

One cupful and a half of uncooked rice, and two dozen apples. Wash the rice well, and soak two hours in cold water. Peel and quarter the apples. Wet the pudding cloth and spread it in the colander. Cover with two-thirds of the rice. Lay in the apples, having them packed as closely as possible. Sprinkle the remainder of the rice over them. Tie as tightly as possible, and plunge into boiling water. Boil one hour. Serve with molasses sauce.

Eve's Pudding.

Six eggs, six apples, six ounces of bread, six ounces of currants, half a teaspoonful of salt, nutmeg. Boil three hours, or steam four. Serve with wine sauce.

Batter and Fruit Pudding.

One pint of milk, one pint of flour, four eggs, one table-spoonful of butter, one teaspoonful of salt, one pint of fruit, pared and quartered, (apples or peaches are best). Beat the eggs well with a spoon, and add the milk to them. Turn part of this mixture on the flour, and beat to a light, smooth batter. Add the remainder of the milk and eggs, and the salt. Butter a pudding dish and pour in the batter. Sprinkle in the fruit. Bake half an hour. Serve with foaming sauce the moment it comes from the oven.

Amherst Pudding.

Three-fourths of a cupful of butter, three-fourths of a pint of sugar, four eggs, five table-spoonfuls of strained apple, the grated rind and the juice of a lemon, and nutmeg and rose-water, if you like. Bake half an hour, in a moderate oven, in a shallow pudding dish that has been lined with a rich pasts, rolled very thin. Let it become partially cooled before serving.

Swiss Pudding.

One tea-cupful of flour, four table-spoonfuls of butter, three of sugar, one pint of milk, five eggs, the rind of a lemon. Grate the rind of the lemon (the yellow part only, remember,) into the milk, which put in the double boiler. Rub the flour and butter together. Pour the boiling milk on this, and return to the boiler. Cook five minutes, stirring the first two. Beat the yolks of the eggs and the sugar together, and stir into the boiling mixture. Remove from the fire immediately. When cold, add the whites of the eggs, beaten to a stiff froth. Have a three-quart mould, well buttered. Turn the mixture into this, and steam forty minutes. Turn on a hot dish, and serve without delay. Creamy sauce, or a tumbler of currant jelly, melted with the juice of two lemons, should be served with it.

Delicate Indian Pudding.

One quart of milk, two heaping table-spoonfuls of Indian meal, four of sugar, one of butter, three eggs, one teaspoonful of salt. Boil the milk in the double boiler. Sprinkle the meal into it, stirring all the while. Cook twelve minutes, stirring often. Beat together the eggs, salt, sugar and half a teaspoonful of ginger. Stir the butter into the meal and milk. Pour this gradually on the egg mixture. Bake slowly one hour.

Indian and Apple Pudding.

One cupful of Indian meal, one cupful of molasses, two quarts of milk, two teaspoonfuls of salt, three table-spoonfuls of butter, or one of finely-chopped suet; one quart of pared and quartered apples (sweet are best, but sour will do), half a teaspoonful of ginger, half a teaspoonful of grated nutmeg. Put the milk on in the double boiler. When it boils, pour it gradually on the meal. Pour into the boiler again and cook half an hour, stirring often. Add the molasses, butter, seasoning and apples. Butter a deep pudding dish, pour the mixture into it, and bake slowly three hours. Make half the rule if the family is small.

COLD PUDDINGS.

Royal Pudding.

One quart of milk, half a cupful of sago, two table-spoonfuls of butter, one tea-cupful of granulated sugar, half a teaspoonful of salt, four eggs, four table-spoonfuls of raspberry jam, four table-spoonfuls of wine. Put the milk in the double boiler, and just before it comes to a boil, stir in the sago. Cook until it thickens (about half an hour), stirring frequently; then add the butter, sugar and salt. Let it cool; and when cold, add the yolks of the eggs, well beaten, and the wine. Turn into a buttered pudding dish, and bake half an hour. Set away to cool. When cold, spread the jam over it. Beat the whites of the eggs to a stiff froth, and stir into them four table-spoonfuls of powdered sugar. Spread this on the pudding. Brown quickly, and serve. The pudding can be made the day before using. In this case, put the whites of the eggs in the ice chest, and make the meringue and brown just before serving.

Cold Tapioca Pudding.

Soak a cupful of tapioca over night in a quart of cold water. In the morning drain off all the water. Put the tapioca and a quart and half a pint of milk in the double boiler. After cooking forty-five minutes, add a teaspoonful of salt Stir well, and cook fifteen minutes longer. Wet a mould or bowl in cold water. Turn the pudding into this, and set away to cool. Serve with sugar and cream. This. pudding is also nice hot.

Danish Pudding.

One cupful of tapioca, three generous pints of water, half a teaspoonful of salt, half a tea-cupful of sugar, one tumbler of any kind of bright jelly. Wash the tapioca, and soak in the water all night. In the morning put on in the double boiler, and cook one hour. Stir frequently. Add the salt, sugar and jelly, and mix thoroughly. Turn into a mould that has been dipped in cold water, and set away to harden. Serve with cream and sugar.

Black Pudding.

One quart of blueberries, one pint of water, one cupful of sugar, a five-cent baker's loaf, butter. Stew the berries, sugar and water together. Cut the bread in thin slices, and butter these. Put a layer of the bread in a deep dish, and cover it with some of the hot berries. Continue this until all the bread and fruit is used, and set away to cool. The pudding should be perfectly cold when served. Serve with cream and sugar. Any other small berries can be used instead of blueberries.

Almond Pudding.

One pint of shelled almonds, two dozen macaroons, the grated rind of a lemon, half a cupful of sugar, half a cupful of butter, the yolks of six eggs, one quart of milk, one pint of cream, one table-spoonful of rice flour. Blanch the almonds and pound them in a mortar. Put the milk in a double boiler, reserving half a cupful. Add the pounded almonds to it. Mix the rice flour with the half cupful of cold milk, and stir into the boiling milk. Cook six minutes, and put away to cool. When about half cooled, add the sugar and butter, which should have been beaten together until light When cold, add the yolks of the eggs, well beaten, the macaroons, which have been dried and rolled fine, and the cream. Butter a pudding dish that will hold a little more than two quarts; or, two small ones will do. Turn the mixture into this, and bake slowly forty-five minutes. Serve cold.

Jenny Lind Pudding.

One dozen sponge fingers, one dozen macaroons, one dozen cocoanut cakes, one quart of custard, two cupfuls of freshly-grated cocoanut. Make a quart of soft custard, and season with one teaspoonful of lemon extract or two table-spoonfuls of wine. When cold, pour on the cakes, which have been arranged in a deep glass dish. Sprinkle the grated cocoanut over this, and serve. If you have not the fresh cocoanut use one cupful of the prepared.

Peach Meringue Pudding.

Three dozen ripe peaches, one and a third cupfuls of granulated sugar, six table-spoonfuls of powdered sugar, one quart of milk, three teaspoonfuls of corn-starch, six eggs. Put one cupful of the granulated sugar and one pint of water on to boil. Peel and quarter the peaches. When the sugar and water begins to boil, put in one-third of the peaches, and simmer eight minutes. Take them up, and put in another third. Continue this until all the fruit is done. Boil the syrup until it becomes thick. Pour over the peaches and set away to cool. Separate the whites and yolks of the six eggs, and put the whites in the ice chest. Beat together the yolks and one-third of a cupful of sugar. Put a pint and a half of milk in the double boiler. Mix three teaspoonfuls of corn-starch with half a pint of cold milk, and when the other milk is boiling, stir this into it Stir for three minutes; then put on the cover and cook three minutes longer. Pour the boiling mixture gradually on the beaten eggs and sugar. Return to the boiler and cook four minutes, stirring all the while. Take from the fire, add half a teaspoonful of salt, and set away to cool. This is the sauce. Twenty minutes before serving heap the peaches in the centre of a shallow dish. Beat the whites of the eggs to a stiff froth, and gradually beat in five table-spoonfuls of powdered sugar. Cover the peaches with this. Place a board in the oven, put the dish on it, and cook until a light brown. Season the sauce with one-fourth of a teaspoonful of almond extract, and pour around the pudding. Serve.

The peaches and sauce must be cold. If the oven is hot, and the board is placed under the dish, the browning of the meringue will not heat the pudding much.

Apple Meringue Pudding.

Two quarts of pared and quartered apples, a lemon, two cupfuls of granulated sugar and six table-spoonfuls of powdered, six eggs, one quart of milk, three teaspoonfuls of corn-starch. Pare the thin yellow rind off of the lemon, being careful not to cut into the white part, and put it in a sauce-pan with one and two-thirds cupfuls of the granulated sugar. Boil ten minutes;

then put in the apples and juice of the lemon. Cover, and simmer half an hour. The apples should be tender, but not much broken. Take them up, and boil the syrup until thick. When it is reduced enough, pour it over the apples, and put these away to cool. Make the sauce and finish the pudding the same as for peach meringue, flavoring the sauce, however, with extract of lemon.

Frozen Cabinet Pudding.

Two dozen stale lady-fingers, one cupful of English currants, one pint of cream, one pint of milk, one *small* tea-cupful of sugar, three eggs, three table-spoonfuls of wine. Put the milk in the double boiler. Beat the eggs and sugar together, and gradually pour the hot milk on them. Return to the boiler and cook two minutes, stirring all the while. Pour the hot custard on the lady-fingers, add the currants, and set away to cool. When cold, add the wine and the cream, whipped to a froth. Freeze the same as ice cream. When frozen, wet a melon mould in cold water, sprinkle a few currants on the sides and bottom, and pack with the frozen mixture. Pack the mould in salt and ice for one hour. At serving time, wipe it, and dip in warm water for a moment Turn out the pudding on a dish, pour apricot sauce around it, and serve.

Frozen Cabinet Pudding, No. 2.

One dozen macaroons, one dozen and a half sponge fingers, one dozen cocoanut cakes, one cupful of English currants, one quart of custard. Wet a melon mould in cold water. Sprinkle the sides and bottom with currants. Arrange layers of the mixed cakes, which sprinkle with currants. Continue this until all the cake and currants are used. Put a pint and a half of milk in the double boiler. Beat together four eggs and two table-spoonfuls of sugar. When the milk is hot, stir in one-third of a package of gelatine, which has been soaking one hour in half a cupful of milk. Add the beaten egg and sugar, and cook four minutes, stirring all the while. Take off, and add one-fourth of a teaspoonful of salt and one teaspoonful of vanilla, or two table-spoonfuls of wine. Pour this, a few spoonfuls at a time, on the cake. Set away to cool. When cold, cover with thick white paper, and put on the tin cover. Pack the mould in salt and ice for four or six hours. At serving time, wipe the mould free of salt and ice and dip for a moment in warm water. Take off the cover and paper, and turn out. Serve with quince sauce.

Peach Pudding.

Pare and cut fine one dozen ripe peaches. Sprinkle with three table spoonfuls of sugar, and let them stand one hour. Make a custard the same as for frozen cabinet pudding, No. 2. Have the peaches in a deep glass dish, and, as soon as the custard is partly cooled, turn it on them. Set away in a cold place for six or eight hours. When convenient, it is well to make this pudding the day before using.

Orange Pudding.

One pint of milk, the juice of six oranges and rind of three, eight eggs, half a cupful of butter, one large cupful of granulated sugar, a quarter of a cupful of powdered sugar, one table-spoonful of ground rice, paste to line the pudding dish. Mix the ground rice with a little of the cold milk. Put the remainder of the milk in the double boiler, and when it boils, stir in the mixed rice. Stir for five minutes; then add the butter, and set away to cool. Beat together the sugar, the yolks of the eight eggs and whites of four. Grate the rind and squeeze the juice of the oranges into this. Stir all into the cooked mixture. Have a pudding dish, holding about three quarts, lined with paste. Pour the preparation into this, and bake in a moderate oven for forty minutes. Beat the remaining four whites of the eggs to a stiff froth, and gradually beat in the powdered sugar. Cover the pudding with this. Return to the oven, and cook ten minutes, having the door open. Set away to cool. It must be ice cold when served.

Orange Pudding, No. 3.

One cupful and a half of granulated sugar, six table-spoonfuls of the powdered, six eggs, six large, or eight small, sweet oranges, half a package of gelatine, one quart of boiling milk. Soak the gelatine for two hours in one cupful of the milk. Put the remaining milk in the double boiler. Beat together the yolks of the eggs and the granulated sugar. When the milk boils, stir in the gelatine, and then the beaten yolks and sugar. Stir constantly until the mixture begins to thicken (which will be about five minutes); then remove from the fire and put away to cool. Pare the oranges, and free them of seeds and tough parts. Put them in a large glass dish, and when the custard has cooled, pour it over the fruit. Let this stand in a cold place six or eight hours. Beat the whites of the eggs to a stiff froth, and gradually beat in the powdered sugar. Cover the pudding with this, and serve.

Royal Diplomatic Pudding.

Soak half a box of gelatine in half a cupful of cold water one or two hours. Pour on this two-thirds of a pint of boiling water, and add the juice of a lemon, a cupful of sugar and half a pint of wine. Stir, and strain. Have two moulds, one holding two quarts, the other a quart. Put a layer of jelly in the large mould, and place on ice. When hard, garnish with candied cherries, cut in two. Pour in a few spoonfuls of liquid jelly, *not hot*, to hold the cherries, and then pour in enough to cover them. When the jelly is perfectly hard, set the small mould in the centre of the large one, and fill the space between with jelly. Fill the small mould with ice, and set both in a basin of ice water. When the jelly is again hard, remove the ice from the small mould, which fill with warm water, and lift it out carefully. The vacant space is to be filled with custard made by the following recipe: The yolks of five eggs, half a cupful of sugar, two table-spoonfuls of wine, one teaspoonful of vanilla extract, half a box of gelatine, soaked in half a cupful of cold water, a scant cupful of milk. Put the milk to boil. Add the gelatine, and the eggs and sugar, beaten together. Strain, and add the wine and vanilla. When the custard begins to thicken, add half a pint of cream, whipped to a stiff froth. Pour the custard into the space mentioned, and let it stand until it hardens. Turn the pudding out of the mould, and serve with soft custard poured around it.

Orange Diplomatic Pudding.

Make one quart of orange jelly. Arrange this in the mould and make a filling the same as for royal diplomatic pudding. Flavor the filling, and the custard for the sauce, with orange.

Lemon Diplomatic Pudding.

Make one quart of lemon jelly, and prepare the mould with it the same as for the royal diplomatic pudding. Make a lemon sponge, with which fill the cavity. When hard, serve with a custard flavored with lemon.

Bird's Nest Pudding.

Half a package of Cox's sparkling gelatine, six oranges, three cupfuls and a half of sugar, one pint of blanc-mange. Take the peel from the oranges in quarters. Put it in two quarts of water, and let it stand over night. In the morning drain off the water. Cut the peel in thin strips with the scissors. Put it in cold water and boil until tender. Make a syrup of half a cupful of sugar and a pint of water. Drain the straws of orange peel on a sieve. Put them in this syrup and simmer half an hour. Turn into a bowl, and let stand until next day. Put one pint of sugar and one pint of water on to boil. Cook rapidly for twenty minutes; the syrup will then fall from the spoon in threads. Put the straws in this and boil half an hour. Take out, and drain on a sieve. As they dry, put them in a dish, which place in the warm oven. These are for the nests. For the jelly, soak the gelatine two hours in half a cupful of cold water; then pour on it enough boiling water to make, with the juice of the oranges, two cupfuls and a half. Add one small cupful of sugar and the orange juice. Stir well, and strain through a napkin into a shallow dish. In one end of each of six eggs make a hole, about the size of a cent Break the yolks with a skewer, and pour the eggs into a bowl. (They may be used for puddings and custards.) Wash and drain the shells. Fill them with the blanc-mange. Have a pan filled with meal, in which to stand the shells. Set away to cool. Break the jelly in pieces with a fork, and put in a flat glass dish. Arrange the straws in the form of nests, six in number, and arrange them on the jelly. Place the eggs in these, and serve.

Quince Iced Pudding.

Beat three eggs very light; then add one cupful and a half of powdered sugar, and beat until foamy. Put two cupfuls of sifted pastry flour in the sieve, and add one teaspoonful of cream of tarter and half a teaspoonful of soda. Stir half a cupful of cold water into the beaten eggs and sugar; then sift the flour on this. Mix quickly and thoroughly. Have a tin mould similar to the border moulds shown in the chapter on Kitchen Furnishing, but of oval shape, higher and plain. It should be about four inches high, and six wide and eight long, top measurement--the mould tapering. The space between the outer and inner walls should be an inch and a half. Butter this mould and pour the cake mixture into it. Bake slowly for forty-five minutes. Let it stand in the mould until nearly cold. Turn on a flat dish. Put the whites of two eggs in a bowl, gradually beat into them one cupful and a half of powdered sugar, and season with half a teaspoonful of vanilla extract Ice the cake with this, and set away to dry. In the meantime, make a cream with one generous quart of cream, one cupful of sugar, one table-spoonful of vanilla and one pint of soft custard. Freeze the same as ice cream. Spread the inside of the cake with a large tumbler of quince jelly. At serving time pack the frozen cream in the centre of the cake. Heap whipped cream on the top and at the base, and serve immediately. This is an elegant pudding, and is not difficult to make.

Princess Pudding.

Soak for an hour in a pint of cold water one box of Cox's sparkling gelatine, and add one pint of boiling water, one pint of wine, the juice of four lemons, and three large cupfuls of sugar. Beat the whites of four eggs to a stiff froth, and stir into the jelly when it begins to thicken. Pour into a large mould, and set in ice water in a cool place. When ready to serve, turn out as you would jelly, only have the pudding in a deep dish. Pour one quart of soft custard around it, and serve.

Apple Porcupine.

Sixteen large apples, two large cupfuls of granulated sugar, one lemon, one quart of water, one tea-cupful of powdered sugar, one quart of milk, one table-spoonful of corn-starch, half a teaspoonful of salt, six eggs, one pint of blanched almonds. Put the water and granulated sugar in a sauce-pan. Have ten of the apples pared and cored, and as soon as the sugar and water boils, put in as many of the apples as will cook without crowding. Simmer gently until the fruit is cooked through. When done on one side the fruit must be turned. Drain, and cool them on a dish. Cook ten apples in this manner. Have the six that remain pared and quartered and stewed in one cupful of water. Turn the stewed apples into the syrup left from cooking the others. Add the grated rind and the juice of the lemon. Simmer until a smooth marmalade is formed. It will take about twenty minutes. Set away to cool. Put the milk on in the double boiler, reserving half a cupful. When it boils, stir in the corn-starch, which has been mixed with the cold milk. Stir well, and cook five minutes. Beat the yolks of the six eggs and the whites of two with half of the powdered sugar. Gradually pour the boiling mixture on this. Return to the boiler and cook three minutes, stirring all the time. Add the salt. Turn into a pitcher or bowl, and set away to cool. Heap the cooked apples in a mound, using the marmalade to fill up the spaces between the apples. Beat the four whites of eggs to a stiff froth, and beat the half cupful of powdered sugar into it. Cover the apples with this, and stick the almonds into it. Brown slowly in the oven. Set away to cool. At serving time, season the custard with lemon, and pour it around the porcupine.

SAUCES.

Rich Wine Sauce.

One cupful of butter, two of powdered sugar, half a cupful of wine. Beat the butter to a cream. Add the sugar gradually, and when very light, add the wine, which has been made hot, a little at a time. Place the bowl in a basin of hot water and stir for two minutes. The sauce should be smooth and foamy.

Creamy Sauce.

Half a cupful of butter, one cupful of *powdered* sugar, one-fourth of a cupful of cream or milk, four table-spoonfuls of wine, or one teaspoonful of vanilla or lemon extract. If lemon or vanilla is used, add four table-spoonfuls of cream. Beat the butter to a cream. Add the sugar, gradually, beating all the while. When light and creamy, gradually add the wine, and then the cream, a little at a time. When all is beaten smooth, place the bowl in a basin of hot water and stir until the sauce is smooth and creamy--no longer. It will take only a few minutes. This is a delicious sauce, and if well beaten, and not kept in the hot water long enough to melt the sugar, it will be white and foamy all through.

Foaming Sauce.

One cupful of butter, two of powdered sugar, the whites of two eggs, five table-spoonfuls of wine or three of brandy, one-fourth of a tea-cupful of *boiling* water. Beat the butter to a cream, and gradually beat the sugar into it. Add the whites of the eggs, unbeaten, one at a time, and then the brandy or wine. When all is a light, smooth mass, add the water, beating in a little at a time. Place the bowl in a basin of hot water and stir until smooth and frothy, which will be about two minutes. This sauce is for rich puddings.

German Sauce.

One cupful of sugar, half a cupful of water, three eggs, one table-spoonful of butter, three of brandy, or a teaspoonful of any extract you like. Put the sugar and water in a sauce-pan and boil for fifteen minutes. Beat the yolks of the eggs, and stir them into the boiling syrup. Put the basin in another of hot water and beat the mixture with the whisk until it begins to thicken; then add the butter, the whites of the eggs, beaten to a stiff froth, and the brandy. Stir one minute longer, and serve.

German Sauce, No. 2.

The yolks of five and whites of three eggs, one cupful of powdered sugar, one pint of cream, and any flavor you choose. Beat together the yolks of the eggs and the sugar, and add the cream. Put this mixture in the double boiler (having first beaten the whites to a stiff froth), and stir until it begins to thicken; then add the whites and seasoning. Beat thoroughly, and serve.

Lemon Sauce.

One cupful of sugar, half a cupful of water, the rind and juice of two lemons, the yolks of three eggs. Boil together the sugar, water, lemon juice and grated rind for twenty minutes. Beat the yolks of the eggs. Put the basin containing the boiling syrup in another of boiling water. Stir the yolks of the eggs into this, and beat rapidly for three minutes. Take up the sauce-pan and continue the beating for five minutes; then serve.

Cream Sauce.

One cupful of powdered sugar, one egg, two cupfuls of whipped cream. Beat the white of the egg to a stiff froth. Add the yolk and sugar, and beat well. Flavor with vanilla, lemon or wine, and add the cream last of all. This sauce is excellent for a light pudding.

Vanilla Sauce.

The whites of two eggs and the yolk of one, half a cupful of powdered sugar, one teaspoonful of vanilla, three table-spoonfuls of milk. Beat the whites of the eggs to a stiff froth, next beat in the sugar, and then the yolk of the egg and the seasoning. Serve immediately. This sauce is for light puddings.

Molasses Sauce.

One cupful of molasses, half a cupful of water, one table-spoonful of butter, a little cinnamon or nutmeg (about half a teaspoonful), one-fourth of a teaspoonful of salt, three table-spoonfuls of vinegar. Boil all together for twenty minutes. The juice of a lemon can be used instead of the vinegar. This sauce is nice for apple or rice puddings.

Caramel Sauce.

Put one cupful of sugar in a small frying-pan and stir on the fire until a dark brown, if you like a strong caramel flavor, or till a light brown, if you like a delicate flavor. Add a cupful of boiling water, and simmer fifteen minutes. Set away to cool.

Quince Sauce.

One cupful of quince preserve, one of milk, one table-spoonful of corn-starch, half a cupful of sugar. Mix the corn-starch with a little of the cold milk, and put the remainder in the double boiler. When it boils, stir in the corn-starch, and cook ten minutes; then add the sugar and the preserve, mashed fine. Cook ten minutes longer and rub through a strainer. This sauce is usually served cold, but when used with hot pudding, it too should be hot.

Apricot Sauce.

One cupful of canned apricot, one of sugar, one of milk, one table-spoonful of corn-starch, half a cupful of water. Put the milk in the double boiler. Mix the corn-starch with a few spoonfuls of cold milk, and stir into the boiling milk. Cook ten minutes. Boil the sugar and water together for twenty minutes. Rub the apricot through a sieve, and stir it into the syrup. Beat well, and then beat in the boiled milk and corn-starch. Place the sauce-pan in a dish of cold water and stir for about eight minutes. Set away to cool. If you have cream, use it instead of the milk. All kinds of fruit can be used in pudding sauces by following this rule. If the fruit is preserved, use less sugar; and if very acid, use more.

If it is necessary to make the wine, creamy or foamy sauce any considerable time before dinner, do not add the hot water or hot wine, and do not place the bowl in hot water, until serving time. The vanilla and cream sauces are spoiled by standing after being made.

DESSERT.

Blanc-Mange Made with Sea Moss Farina.

One quart of milk, one level table-spoonful of sea moss farina, half a teaspoonful of salt, three table-spoonfuls of sugar, one teaspoonful of flavor. Put the milk in the double boiler and sprinkle the farina into it, stirring all the while. Let this heat slowly. Stir often. When it boils up, and looks white, add the sugar, salt and flavor. Strain, and turn into a mould that has been dipped in cold water. Set away to harden. It will take about three hours for this. The blanc-mange is ready to use as soon as cold.

Blanc-Mange Made with Gelatine.

One package of gelatine, three pints of milk, four table-spoonfuls of sugar, half a teaspoonful of salt, one teaspoonful of extract of vanilla or of lemon. Put the gelatine with the milk and let it stand in a cold place for two hours; then put it in the double boiler, and heat quickly. Do not let it boil. Stir often; and as soon as the gelatine is melted, take off, and add the sugar, salt and flavor. Strain, and partially cool, before putting into the moulds. It should stand six hours before serving, and it is even better, especially in summer, to make it the day before using.

Blanc-Mange Made with Isinglass.

One quart of milk, three and a half sheets of Cooper's isinglass, half a teaspoonful of salt, three table-spoonfuls of sugar and a four-inch piece of stick cinnamon. Break up the isinglass, put it and the cinnamon with the milk, and let stand in a cold place two hours; then put it in the double boiler and let it come, gradually, to the boiling point. It must not boil. Stir often while heating. As soon as the isinglass is dissolved, take from the fire, and add the salt and sugar. Strain into a tin basin, which place in a pan of cold water. Stir occasionally while cooling. When nearly cold, turn into a mould and place in the ice chest. It can be poured into the mould as soon as strained, but the cream will rise to the top in that case, unless the mixture is stirred carefully in the centre of the mould. The sheets of isinglass vary in thickness, so that it is best to take part of die thick sheets and part of the thin.

Chocolate "Blanc"-Mange.

One package of gelatine, four table-spoonfuls of sugar, one (ounce) square of Baker's chocolate, three pints of milk. Soak the gelatine two hours in the milk, and then put it in the double boiler. Scrape the chocolate fine and put it in a small frying-pan with two spoonfuls of the sugar and two of boiling water. Stir this over a *hot* fire until smooth and glossy (it will take about a minute), and stir into the milk. Add the remainder of the sugar, and strain. Turn into moulds, and set away to harden. This dish should be made at least eight hours before being used. If you please, you can add a teaspoonful of vanilla extract. By adding the chocolate to any of the preparations for blanc-mange while they are hot, you have a chocolate "blanc"-mange.

Cream à la Versailles.

One quart of milk, half a cupful of sugar, half a teaspoonful of vanilla extract, half a teaspoonful of salt, seven eggs, two table-spoonfuls of water. Put the sugar in a small frying-pan and stir until a very light brown. Add the water, stir a moment longer, and mix with the milk. Beat the eggs and salt with a spoon. Add this mixture and the vanilla to the milk. Butter a two-quart charlotte russe mould lightly, and put the custard in it Put the mould in a basin of warm (not hot) water and bake slowly until the custard is firm in the centre. It should take forty minutes; but if the oven is quite hot, it will be done in thirty minutes. Test by putting a knife down into the centre, for if the custard is not milky, it is done. Set away in a cold place until serving time. It must be ice cold when eaten. Turn out on a flat dish, and pour caramel sauce over it.

Royal Cream.

One quart of milk, one-third of a box of gelatine, four table-spoonfuls of sugar, three eggs, vanilla flavor. Put the gelatine in the milk, and let it stand for half an hour. Beat the yolks well with sugar, and stir into the milk. Set the kettle in a pan of hot water and stir until the mixture begins to thicken like soft custard. Have ready the whites of the eggs, beaten to a stiff froth; and the moment the kettle is taken from the fire, stir them in, quickly, and turn into the moulds. Set away in a cold place to harden.

When you cannot get cream, to make charlotte russe, this is a good filling, if you omit the whites of eggs, and fill the moulds when the cream is perfectly cold, but not hardened.

Lemon Sponge.

The juice of four lemons, four eggs, one cupful of sugar, half a package of gelatine, one generous pint of cold water. Soak the gelatine two hours in half a cupful of the water. Squeeze the lemons, and strain the juice on the sugar. Beat the yolks of the eggs and mix them with the remainder of the water. Add the sugar and lemon to this, and cook in the double boiler until it begins to thicken; then add the gelatine. Strain this mixture into a tin basin, which place in a pan of ice water. Beat with the whisk occasionally, until it has cooled, but not hardened. Now add the unbeaten whites of the eggs, and beat all the time until the mixture begins to thicken. Let it thicken almost to the point where it cannot be poured, and then turn into a mould and set away to harden. Remember that the whites of the eggs must be added as soon as the mixture cools, which should be in about six or eight minutes, and that the mixture must be beaten until it begins to harden. The hardening is rapid after it once begins, so that it will be necessary to have the moulds all ready. The sponge will not be smooth and delicate if not poured into the moulds. If for any reason you should get the mixture too hard before pouring, place the basin in another of hot water, and let the sponge melt a little; then beat it up again. Serve with powdered sugar and cream.

Orange Sponge.

Make orange sponge the same as lemon, using a small pint of water and the juice of six large oranges.

Peach Sponge.

One pint of canned peaches, half a package of gelatine, the whites of five eggs, one scant cupful of sugar, one and a half cupfuls of water. Soak the gelatine for two hours in half a cupful of the water. Boil the cupful of water, and the sugar fifteen minutes. Hash the peaches fine, rub through a sieve, and put in the syrup. Cook five minutes, stirring all the time. Place the sauce-pan in another of boiling water and add the gelatine. Stir for five or eight minutes, to dissolve the gelatine; then place the sauce-pan in a dish of ice water and beat the syrup until it begins to cool. Add the whites of the eggs, and beat until the mixture begins to harden. When it will just pour, turn it into the mould, and set away to harden. Serve with sugar and cream. Apricot and pear sponges can be made in the same manner.

Strawberry Sponge.

One quart of strawberries, half a package of gelatine, one cupful and a half of water, one cupful of sugar, the juice of a lemon, the whites of four eggs. Soak the gelatine two hours in half a cupful of the water. Mash the strawberries, and add half the sugar to them. Boil the remainder of the sugar and the cupful of water gently twenty minutes. Rub the strawberries through a sieve. Add the gelatine to the boiling syrup and take from the fire immediately; then add the strawberries. Place in a pan of ice water and beat five minutes. Add the whites of eggs and beat until the mixture begins to thicken. Pour into the moulds and set away to harden. Serve with sugar and cream. Raspberry and blackberry sponges are made in the same way.

Pineapple Sponge.

One small fresh pineapple, or a pint-and-a-half can of the fruit; one small cupful of sugar, half a package of gelatine, one cupful and a half of water, the whites of four eggs. Soak the gelatine two hours in half a cupful of the water. Chop the pineapple, and put it and the juice in a sauce-pan with the sugar and the remainder of the water. Simmer ten minutes. Add the gelatine, take from the fire immediately, and strain into a tin basin. When partially cooled, add the whites of the eggs, and beat until the mixture begins to thicken. Pour into a mould and set away to harden. Serve with soft custard flavored with wine.

Strawberry Bavarian Cream.

One quart of strawberries, one pint of cream, one large cupful of sugar, half a cupful of boiling water, half a cupful of cold water. Soak the gelatine two hours in the cold water. Mash the berries and sugar together, and let them stand one hour. Whip the cream to a froth. Strain the juice from the berries, pressing through as much as possible without the seeds. Pour the hot water on the gelatine, and when dissolved, strain it into the strawberry juice. Place the basin (which should be tin) in a pan of ice water and beat until the cream begins to thicken. When as thick as soft custard, stir in the whipped cream; and when this is well mixed, turn into the mould (it will make nearly two quarts), and set away to harden. Serve with whipped cream heaped around it, or, if the border mould is used, have the cream in the centre.

Raspberry and blackberry Bavarian creams are made the same as the strawberry.

Orange Bavarian Cream.

A pint and a half of cream, the juice of five oranges and grated rind of two, one large cupful of sugar, the yolks of six eggs, half a package of gelatine, half a cupful of cold water. Soak the gelatine two hours in the cold water. Whip the cream, and skim off until there is less than half a pint unwhipped. Grate the rind of the oranges on the gelatine, Squeeze and strain the orange juice, and add the sugar to it. Put the unwhipped cream in the double boiler. Beat the yolks of the eggs and add to the milk. Stir this mixture until it begins to thicken, and add the gelatine. As soon as the gelatine is dissolved, take off, and place in a pan of ice water. Stir until it begins to cool (about two minutes), and add the orange juice and sugar. Beat about as thick as soft custard, and add the whipped cream. Stir until well mixed, and pour into the moulds. Set away to harden. There will be about two quarts. Serve with whipped cream heaped around the orange cream.

Peach Bavarian Cream.

One quart of canned peaches, one large cupful of sugar, one pint of cream, half a box of gelatine, half a cupful of cold water. Mash the peaches and rub them and the juice through a sieve. Add the sugar. Soak the gelatine two hours in the cold water. Whip the cream to a froth. Put the peaches in a sauce-pan and let them simmer twenty minutes. Stir often. Add the gelatine to the hot peaches and remove from the fire immediately. Place the sauce-pan in a pan of ice water and beat until the mixture begins to thicken; then stir in the cream. Mix thoroughly, and pour into the mould. Set away to harden. Serve with whipped cream. Apricot and pear Bavarian creams are made in the same way.

Pineapple Bavarian Cream.

One pint of canned pineapple, one small tea-cupful of sugar, one pint of cream, half a package of gelatine, half a cupful of cold water. Soak the gelatine two hours in the water. Chop the pineapple fine and put it on with the sugar. Simmer twenty minutes. Add the gelatine, and strain immediately into a tin basin. Rub as much of the pineapple as possible through the sieve. Beat until it begins to thicken, and add the cream, which has been whipped to a froth. When well mixed, pour into the mould, and put away to harden. Serve with whipped cream.

Almond Bavarian Cream.

One pint and a half of cream, one pint of blanched sweet almonds, one-fourth of a teaspoonful of essence of almond, half a package of gelatine, three eggs, one small cupful of sugar, half a cupful of milk. Soak the gelatine two hours in the milk. Whip the cream to a stiff froth, until about half a pint is left unwhipped. Pound the almonds to a paste in the mortar.

Put the almonds and unwhipped cream in the double boiler. Beat the sugar and eggs together and stir in with the cream and almonds. Cook until the mixture begins to thicken; then stir in the gelatine, and remove from the fire. Strain this into a tin basin, and add the essence of almond. Beat until it begins to thicken, and add the whipped cream. Mix well, pour into the moulds, and set away. Serve with whipped cream. Pistachio Bavarian cream is made in the same way, using one pint of pistachio nuts instead of the almonds, and omitting the essence of almond.

Chocolate Bavarian Cream.

One pint of cream, one cupful of milk, half a cupful of sugar, half a box of gelatine, one square of Baker's chocolate (an ounce). Soak the gelatine in half a cupful of the milk. Whip the cream to a stiff froth. Scrape the chocolate, and add two table-spoonfuls of the sugar to it. Put in a small frying-pan with one table-spoonful of hot water. Stir over a hot fire until smooth and glossy. Have the remaining half cupful of milk boiling. Stir the chocolate into it, and add the gelatine. Strain into a tin basin, and add the remainder of the sugar. Place the basin in a pan of ice water and beat the mixture until it begins to thicken; then add the whipped cream; and when well mixed, turn into the mould. When hard, serve with whipped cream heaped around.

Coffee Bavarian Cream.

One cupful of strong coffee, one pint of cream, half a package of gelatine, one cupful of sugar, one-third of a cupful of cold water. Soak the gelatine two hours in the cold water. Pour on this the coffee, boiling hot, and when the gelatine is dissolved, add the sugar. Strain into a tin basin, which put in a pan of ice water. Beat with a whisk until it begins to thicken; then add the cream, which has been whipped to a froth. When thoroughly mixed, turn into a mould and set away to harden. Serve with sugar and cream.

Directions for Freezing.

Four the mixture that is to be frozen into the tin can, put the beater in this, and put on the cover. Place in the tub, being careful to have the point on the bottom fit into the socket in the tub. Put on the cross-piece, and turn the crank to see if everything is in the right place. Next comes the packing. Ice should be broken in large pieces, and put in a canvas bag, and pounded fine with a mallet. Put a thick layer of it in the tub (about five inches deep), and then a thin layer of salt. Continue this until the tub is full, and pack down solid with a paddle or a common piece of wood. After turning the crank a few times add more salt and ice, and again pack down. Continue in this way until the tub is full. For a gallon can, three pints of salt and perhaps ten quarts of fine ice will be required. Remember that if the freezer is packed solid at first, no more ice or salt is needed. The water must never be let off, as it is one of the strongest elements to help the freezing. If more salt than the quantity given is used, the cream will freeze sooner, but it will not be so smooth and rich as when less is used.

Turn the crank for twenty minutes--not fast at first, but very rapidly the last ten minutes. It will be hard to torn when the mixture is frozen. Turn back the cross-piece, wipe the salt and ice from the cover, and take off the cover, not displacing the can itself. Remove the beater and scrape the cream from it. Work a large spoon up and down in the cream until it is light and the space left by taking out the beater is filled. Cover the can, cork up the hole from which the handle of the beater was taken, put on the cross piece, and set the tub in a cool place until serving time. Then dip the can for a few seconds in water that is a trifle warm, wipe it, and turn on the dish. Rest it for a moment, and lift a little.

If the cream is to be served from a mould, remove it when you do the beater. Fill the mould and work the cream up and down with a spoon. This will press the cream into every part, and lighten it. Cover the top of the mould with thick white paper, put on the tin cover, and bury in fresh ice and salt.

There are a great many good freezers. The Packer is especially suited to family use. It turns so easily that any lady can make her own creams. For the first twelve minutes a child can work it. It is made of the best stock, and will last many years. The cogs on freezers should be oiled occasionally. When you have made cream, see that every part of the freezer is clean and perfectly dry before putting away.

Vanilla Ice Cream.

The foundation given in this rule is suitable for all kinds of ice cream. One generous pint of milk, one cupful of sugar, half a cupful of flour, *scant*; two eggs, one quart of cream, one table-spoonful of vanilla extract, and when the cream is added, another tea-cupful of sugar. Let the milk come to a boil. Beat the first cupful of sugar, the flour and eggs together, and stir into the boiling milk. Cook twenty minutes, stirring often. Set away to cool, and when cool add the sugar, seasoning and cream, and freeze.

Vanilla Ice Cream, No. 2.

One pint of sugar, one of water, three pints of cream--not too rich, the yolks of five eggs and one large table-spoonful of vanilla extract Boil the sugar and water together for twenty-five minutes. Beat the yolks of the eggs with one-fourth of a teaspoonful of salt Place the basin of boiling syrup in another of boiling water. Stir the yolks of the eggs into the syrup, and beat rapidly for three minutes. Take the basin from the fire, place it in a pan of ice water and beat until cold. Add the vanilla and cream, and freeze.

Lemon Ice Cream.

Make the same as vanilla cream, and flavor with one table-spoonful of lemon extract.

Lemon Ice Cream, No. 2.

Three tea-cupfuls of sugar, the juice of three lemons, three pints of cream, the yolks of eight eggs, one pint of water. Boil the water, sugar and lemon juice together twenty minutes; then proceed as directed for vanilla ice cream, No. 2.

Orange Ice Cream.

Follow the second rule for lemon cream, but use the juice of six oranges instead of that of lemons.

Pineapple Ice Cream.

Make the same as vanilla, and flavor with a teaspoonful of extract of pineapple.

Pineapple Ice Cream, No. 2.

Pare a pineapple and cut it fine. Put it in a sauce-pan with one pint of water and a scant pint of sugar. Simmer gently for thirty minutes. Rub through a sieve, add the cream, gradually, and freeze.

Strawberry Ice Cream.

One quart of cream, one quart of strawberries, one pint of sugar. Mash the sugar and strawberries together, and let them stand one or two hours. Add the cream, rub through a strainer into the freezer, and freeze. Or, the cream can be made the same as the vanilla cream, and when half frozen, the whole berries be stirred in.

Strawberry Ice Cream à la Surprise.

Put three pints of strawberries in a deep dish with one cupful of sugar. Season three pints of cream with a cupful and a half of sugar and two table-spoonfuls of wine. Freeze this. Take out the beater and draw the frozen cream to the sides of the freezer. Fill the space in the centre with the strawberries and sugar, which cover with the frozen cream. Put on the cover and set away for an hour or more. When the cream is turned out, garnish the base, if you please, with strawberries.

Raspberry Ice Cream.

Make raspberry ice cream the same as strawberry, using a little less sugar.

Apricot Ice Cream.

One quart of cream, one generous pint of canned apricot, one pint of sugar, the yolks of three eggs, one pint of water. Boil the sugar and water together twenty minutes. Rub the apricot through a sieve and add it to the boiling syrup; add also the beaten yolks of the eggs, and cook for six minutes, stirring all the while. Take from the fire and place in a pan of cold water.

Beat the mixture ten minutes. If cold at the end of that time, add the cream, and freeze.

Peach Ice Cream.

Peach ice cream can be made like the apricot, having the pint of peaches a very generous one.

Banana Ice Cream.

Make this the same as the apricot, using, however, only one cupful and a half of sugar, and six bananas. More bananas can be used if a strong flavor of the fruit is liked.

Chocolate Ice Cream.

Make a foundation with two eggs, one cupful of sugar, half a cupful of flour and a pint of milk, the same as for vanilla ice cream. While this is cooking, scrape one square (an ounce) of Baker's chocolate, and add to it two table-spoonfuls of sugar and one of boiling water. Stir this over the fire until perfectly smooth and glossy, and add it to the boiling mixture. This quantity gives a very delicate flavor. If a stronger one is wished use two squares of the chocolate. Put the mixture in cold water to cool. Stir occasionally. When cold, add one tea-cupful of sugar and one quart of milk. Freeze.

Brown Bread Ice Cream.

Dry the crust of brown bread in a warm oven. Roll fine and sift. Add one pint of the crumbs to the preparation for vanilla ice cream. The vanilla, and two-thirds of the second cupful of sugar must be omitted.

Macaroon Ice Cream.

Make a cream the same as for vanilla, except omit the second cupful of sugar and the vanilla flavor. Brown one dozen and a half macaroons into the oven. Let them cool; then roll them into fine crumbs. Add these and three table-spoonfuls of wine to the cream, and freeze.

Coffee Ice Cream.

Make the same as vanilla, with the addition of one cupful of strong coffee. This gives a strong flavor. Less can be used. The second cupful of sugar should be large.

Caramel Ice Cream.

Make the hot mixture, as for vanilla. Put the small cupful of sugar in a small frying-pan and stir over the fire until the sugar turns liquid and begins to smoke. Turn into the boiling mixture, and put away to cool. When cold, add one quart of cream. Strain the mixture into the freezer, and freeze. The flavor of this cream can be varied by browning the sugar more or less.

Almond Ice Cream.

This is made the same as vanilla, except that one teaspoonful of extract of bitter almond is used for flavoring.

Almond Ice Cream, No. 2.

One pint of blanched almonds, the yolks of five eggs, one quart of cream, one and a half cupfuls of sugar, one pint of milk, one pint of water. Boil the water and sugar together for twenty-five minutes. Put the almonds in a frying-pan and stir over the fire until they are a rich brown. Remove from the fire, and pound to a paste in the mortar. Cook the milk and powdered almonds in the double boiler for twenty minutes. Beat the yolks of the eggs and stir them into the boiling syrup. Beat this for four minutes, having the basin in boiling water. Take from the fire, and gradually beat into it the almonds and milk. Strain the mixture through a sieve, and rub through as much as possible. Stir occasionally while cooling. When cold, add the cream and half a teaspoonful of extract of almond. Freeze.

Pistachio Ice Cream.

One pint of pistachio nuts, half a cupful of blanched almonds, one quart of cream, one pint of water, one scant pint of sugar, the yolks of five eggs, one pint of milk, spinach green enough to give a delicate color (about a heaping teaspoonful-to be cooked with the nuts). Make the same as almond cream.

www.ingramcontent.com/pod-product-compliance
Lightning Source LLC
Chambersburg PA
CBHW081624100526

44590CB00021B/3592